HONORABLY
DISHONORED

Michael French

NEWMAN SPRINGS PUBLISHING
320 Broad Street
Red Bank, NJ 07701

First originally published by Newman Springs Publishing 2021

ISBN 978-1-63881-256-2 (Paperback)
ISBN 978-1-63692-689-6 (Hardcover)
ISBN 978-1-63692-690-2 (Digital)

Printed in the United States of America

ACKNOWLEDGMENTS

The list below contains the people who treated me with respect and really cared for me. They honored me and honored the Hippocratic Oath they took.

Nashville, Tennessee, Veteran's Administration

Chief psychiatrist in 2010 that examined me, thanks for your honesty and care.

Dr. Small, psychiatrist, you pulled me through a lot. You are a great psychiatrist and an asset to this world. Thank you.

Dr. Byrd, dentist, thank you for being so professional. My jawbone goes out to you.

Dr. Byron, podiatrist, as a fellow musician, you are the best.

Kim, in Release of Information, when I asked for your help on my records, you worked with God speed. You are so professional. Thanks.

Lady doctor that operated on my throat in 2009, I am sorry I can't remember your name at this time, and if it wasn't for you, I would not be able to speak. I still have problems. Maybe I will meet you in Chicago. Thank you and God bless you.

Tucson, Arizona, Veteran's Administration

Dr. Lees, primary doctor and most caring and honest man.

Rosemary, Release of Information, so many times you have helped me.

Nate, Eligibility/Enrollment, thanks for the private conversations.

Karen Hauser, ER, you took a lot of pain away from me. Thank you.

Joe, Travel Pay, thanks for all of your help and directions.

May God bless all of these people!

And I want to give special thanks to a woman who is very dear to me and endured all of these things in this book that happened to me from 2012 onward. She also surrendered her time to help me write this book. She went through and survived the pain and witnessed every situation that I went through. She is my fiancé and soul mate. This great woman is Stephanie.

I love you and God Bless You Stephanie.

Love, Michael French

This book is true and straight from my heart, ever since I was fourteen until I was sixty-two years old. I am writing about the wonderful and precious years when I was a child living in Chicago and working and experiencing a great life up until seventeen years of age and still a child, entering the Marine Corps, boot camp in Parris Island. After four years in the Marine Corps, from 1973 to 1977, I was home again in Chicago but now so injured from boot camp I couldn't get rid of it. The feelings, the agony, the stress, the dreams—I am going to climb into your mind as you read this book. Feel this book, and my experiences will belong to you. Even from 2013 until 2018, my tears will be yours.

Sincerely,

Michael French

INTRODUCTION

Testimony: Michael R. French, USMC Boot Camp, June to September 1973

On June 6, 1973, I entered boot camp at Parris Island for the USMC. Two or three weeks into boot camp, it was exposed that I have an allergy to penicillin. The allergic reaction caused me to be hospitalized a couple weeks where I was in a coma and took some time to recover.

Upon release from the hospital, I was reassigned to a new platoon, #257, with the main DI being Sergeant Johnson. DI Sergeant Johnson seemed to single me out as I was the only recruit from the Chicago area while he claimed to also be from the same area. The other recruits in Platoon #257 were all from Virginia.

Being singled out, DI Sergeant Johnson was very excessive in his daily harassment of me. Some incidents include hitting me with the stock of a rifle in the solar plexus and other body parts, hitting me in the head with my footlocker after commanding me to lay on the floor, and many other daily beatings. On one occasion, I was ordered to clean the head and went in with my bath shower shoes and skivvies. DI Sergeant Johnson claimed I was not doing it fast enough and started kicking me on various parts of my body. He ordered me to do push-ups in the head and proceeded to sodomize me in my rectum with a baton-like wooden object while I was prone in the push-up position.

This continued until DI Sergeant Johnson commanded me to return to squad bay and stand at attention. While only in my bath shoes and skivvies, other recruits were present and witnessed the blood that was on my boxers. On another occasion, I was commanded to stand at attention after chow and was distracted by a television broadcast or something that made me turn my head. DI Sergeant Johnson slapped me on the side of the head so hard, I saw stars. DI Sergeant Johnson then proceeded to order me to return to my bottom bunk where he commanded me to put both feet on the top steel bunk, put my head and arms on the concrete floor, and he made me pretend I was changing channels on the dials. I was kept in this position for an hour or more.

On another occasion, during a PT run, I overheated and got sick, which caused me to stop and throw up in mid-run. It was caused by the salt tabs added to our water canteens to prevent dehydration. DI Sergeant Johnson then kicked me repeatedly very hard in the stomach, stating he "wanted to be sure all of the salt tabs were gone so I could continue the run."

On yet another occasion, we were on the rifle range in the prone shooting position on our bellies. DI Sergeant Johnson came up behind me, put his foot in my crotch, and proceeded to step on my testicles. He did not move and stated, "If you miss one shot, you will never have babies again." On another occasion for training in gas mask usage or attacks, we were in the gas chamber and told to take a very deep breath before removing our masks. After removing the mask, we were to give our name, rank, and serial number.

Another training step that was required was for us to clear the mask of any gas and replace it on our heads for continued use. Before I could do this, DI Sergeant Johnson grabbed the mask from my hands and proceeded to put it over my head, backwards, choking me and forcing me to breath in the gas that was not cleared from the mask. The choking continued until I thought I was going to pass out. When the mask was removed, I was coughing and gagging and then pushed out the door where I continued to cough and gag for many minutes.

A nightly event from DI Sergeant Johnson was to approach my bunk after our bedtime prayer to "hope for war with China," and the DI claimed he did not hear my prayer. This resulted in blows to my stomach or other body parts and went on during all of my basic training with this DI. I was subjected to this and similar incidents for a total of ten to eleven weeks before graduation from the USMC Parris Island Boot Camp.

One or more other recruits pressed for an investigation and/or charges for these unorthodox abuses by DI Sergeant Johnson with myself and several others being ordered to stay at Parris Island to submit our testimony against him after graduation from boot camp.

Being forced to stay left me with extra KP duty while waiting for the trial/hearing. While on the extended stay in Parris Island and KP duty, I was repeatedly threatened by

USMC personnel and/or recruits that if I testify against DI Sergeant Johnson, I would never leave Parris Island alive. During this time, I was also assaulted at my bunk with the bunk being flipped, hot water poured over me while sleeping, banging on doors and the steel bunk while sleeping, etc.

Being only seventeen years of age at the time, these actions left me scared to death. I contemplated suicide, disappearing into the swamps surrounding Parris Island, or finding any means possible to leave boot camp. I threw up chow regularly during these times due to the extreme stress, fear, and debasing caused by DI Sergeant Johnson.

In retrospect, these events have caused me to be rebellious and not trusting of any other human being outside of my immediate family for all of my adult years. I voluntarily joined the USMC to serve my country and be one of "the few, the proud, the Marines." I served out my term as a Marine, but the tremendous negative impact to my life caused by these situations continues to make me question if I made the right decision.

1

Feeling Alive
Nothing Bad Could Ever Happen

What a spectacular time in 1972 for me, Michael French, and everything around me in the Chicagoland area. All the way from Lakeshore Drive to Romeoville, Illinois. The sky was blue, white clouds, cool breeze, picnics in the forest preserves, fishing, softball, and we can't forget about the Chicago Cubs or the Bears. Picnics in the backyard, washing the car in the driveway, friends stopping by on their bikes, saying hi—this was the wonder years for me.

I started working at McDonalds at a buck thirty an hour at the age of fourteen from junior high with a work permit from the school signed by my parents. I was not supposed to work past seven o'clock, but my manager George would punch me out and still pay me to work later. I wanted to buy extra things that my parents couldn't afford. Plus, it made me feel important to have a job at that time. I did keep my grades up above average as I was working.

I also gave my mother money that I later found out she saved in her dresser drawer for me. I thought I was contributing to the household expenses, but since Dad was working at Fisher Body General Motors. I guess she felt that it was not needed for the expenses. I think she was trying to teach me responsibilities, which she did.

Back then, our three-bedroom, two-bath house, one-car garage in 1965 only cost $15,900. That's way different from nowadays. I checked the same house on Realtor.com in July 2019. It was about $185,000. That is a great big difference in our economy nowadays. But back to the simple days, stamps were about two cents, gas was about eighty cents a gallon or less.

Things were simple, but times were still difficult. The war was going on in Vietnam, and I was told by the army my draft number was coming up. In fact, it was on television, and letters came out they needed to send more men over, so at that time, I was worried. Then my high school started a forty-five fifteen-day plan with A, B, C, D tracks, which meant when we came back to school since it was overcrowded with nearby communities that I may be starting on A track. Then you may be starting two weeks later on B track, then whoever may be starting on C track two weeks later, then whoever may be starting on D track all year round with no summer vacation. *Well, that really screwed everyone's summer jobs to hell!*

My parents signed for me to buy a 1972 Plymouth 340 Duster. State Farm Insurance at full coverage was $165 every six months. The payments on the car were $110.97 every month. That was pretty hard on a buck thirty an hour. No more summer job, and I was already working every day after school anyway. My job was twenty miles away from my home, which was a gas expense also. That would not let me pay for everything properly, so then I thought about the army recruiter.

As I went down to Afees in Chicago, a Marine Corps recruiter came out and talked to me in front of the army recruiter. He grabbed me by the arm and promised me that if I join the Marine Corps on a delayed entry program because I was only sixteen at the time that I would get college training since I wasn't graduating from high school yet, and tech training for something to take care of me when I got out of the service. He also told me to observe the type of uniform that he was wearing compared to the army which did, in fact, look better. Staff Sergeant Kennedy, the recruiter in Joliet, was wearing dress blues, and they sure did look nice. He had a louder, more commanding, and more convincing voice. As the army recruiter backed down, I chose to listen to the Marine Corps recruiter. I was told and did, in fact, enlist in a six-month delayed entry program and became an honorary recruiter myself, even before boot camp, and I was proud of it.

This is to certify that

Pvt. M. R. FRENCH

is an

HONORARY RECRUITER

for the

UNITED STATES MARINE CORPS

06 April 19 73

NAVMC 6649

USMC Recruiting Service

Honorary Recruiter

With this recruiting badge, I was told to walk twenty miles for the walk of mankind. I was the only one to finish the walk before entering boot camp. With blood and blisters on my toes and feet, I'm the only one that finished the walk. It took several hours and a whole day's time to walk the twenty miles.

I walked hard and I walked proud. I had to finish and I did. I got a little certificate made out of paper with Snoopy—the Charlie Brown Snoopy—lying on top of his doghouse, just a copied off paper stating, "Walk of Mankind," and a Marine Corps sweatshirt to wear while I was walking. But that was okay; at least I did it. I don't know if this helped Staff Sergeant Kennedy recruit more teenagers like myself into the Marine Corps I'm sure now that's what his intentions were. He also brought me around to many schools to speak about the delayed entry program and my guaranteed schooling program.

2

Scared to Death

Now was the time on June 6, 1973, that I was supposed to report to boot camp. Early in the morning of June 6, Afees in Chicago is where my dad dropped me off. He stood and watched as the bus drove away to the airport. There were many types of teenagers on that bus. We were all scared and did not know what was in store for us. I remember on a propjet plane in Charleston, South Carolina, where they told us to hold on because the plane had to land with a flat tire. The plane stopped on the runway. We were told to disembark as they fixed the tire.

It was pretty exciting, and the Charleston, South Carolina, air was humid and warm but kind of breath-taking. This is part of the country that I've never experienced that was kind of swampy, but I was excited. We were then transported from there to Parris Island, South Carolina.

I remember seeing the guard gates and the guards waving the bus through. When the bus stopped, the driver just froze, and a drill instructor with a Smokey the Bear hat came on the bus and started screaming to the top of his lungs, stating, "Hurry, hurry, hurry, you maggots!" And he guided us to painted footprints on the asphalt that we were supposed to stand on. I thought to myself, *This isn't training, it's confusion.*

We were all scared to death. I kept seeing signs like "Only a few good men will succeed here." Also, I saw signs that said, "Death before dishonor." We were told to be at attention or what we thought attention should be, but I guess it wasn't the right way because several of us got hit, beaten, and screamed at. From there, we were hustled into the barbershop to get completely bald haircuts. Then we hustled from there to box our civilian clothes, take showers, and some kind of chemical thrown on our body to kill whatever they thought we might have brought with us. We hustled from there to get three sets of skivvies, three sets of utilities (which are the green khaki uniforms), three sets of green socks, three sets of black nylon dress socks, web belts, two covers, our hats, two pairs of combat boots, one pair of dress shoes, shoe polish, a brass cleaner, Bo-Peep Ammonia, and the rest of our articles. And then we hustled to what they called the bam. I found out later it was actually a squad bay.

We were issued a footlocker, two sheets and pillow cases, pillows, and one wool green military blanket. We had to square everything away in the footlocker to a tee and make our bunks before lunch chow. After ten minutes of eating lunch, we were hustled out of there and sent over to get shots. I can't remember how many shots I took, but I knew I started feeling funny about two hours later. I couldn't or wouldn't say anything at that time because of fear. Plus, we had to go out right away for a three-mile PT run.

I kept feeling like I was going to pass out during the PT and the three-mile runs. Sometimes I would break out in a sweat; both of my knees were about the size of bowling balls. Finally, I asked to go to the doctor. I was laughed at, yelled at, and called a sick bay commando. So I tried to endure this for a week or so. I remember going to sick bay, and all of the recruits that were in sick bay at the time had to stand at attention in a line next to the bulkheads or walls to see the doctors. I remember sliding down the wall, passing out, and that was it.

Approximately a week later, I woke up in the hospital with doctors and nurses all around me. I tried to speak but I could not. I looked up at the ceiling, and it just kept spinning. This happened all that day, and I kept hearing the doctors tell the nurses or other doctors that my vital signs were still unstable. I did not know what was happening at this point. The very next day, I woke up as they were sponge-bathing me. I asked a nurse what was happening. She said the doctor would be in shortly.

I kept asking them, "Where am I? And why am I in here?" Finally, a team of doctors came in. They all had clipboards and were looking at the machines, writing things down, and talking amongst each other. I kept asking, "What's going on?" No one would answer me.

I was so weak, but I managed to knock over a water pitcher so I could get their attention. Finally, I guess it was the head doctor who came over next to me as the nurses was cleaning up the water and told me I had been in a coma. I think he said five days and that I was still in Parris Island hospital. He said they had to run more tests on me, and they did not know if I would be able to go back to training until they had the findings from the tests. I asked anybody if my parents knew what was going on with me. They said everything was taken care of, but really, it was not because this was the only thing they sent my parents: one letter from Parris Island and one letter from Staff Sergeant James W. Kennedy, my recruiter.

I know this is a fact because after they told me what was happening with me being in a coma and that it could be from penicillin, they sent me to a recovery area with other marines. I had a chance to call my mom collect. She did not even know I was in the hospital, much less in a coma. She called up someone at Parris Island and demanded to know what was going on with me. No one could tell her anything or even if they knew me.

After she called all over the Parris Island base, she finally called the hospital and spoke with someone where I was at. I don't know if this move or what my mom did was good or bad. What I mean is I know it's great for a parent to worry about her child, but the doctors and the staff became very bitter with me after that. Within a couple of days, which would have made a total of about two weeks of hospitalization, they told me it was time to sign out and go to a new platoon, which was Platoon #257.

UNITED STATES MARINE CORPS
HEADQUARTERS, MARINE CORPS RECRUIT DEPOT
PARRIS ISLAND, SOUTH CAROLINA 29905

Dear Friends,

The Commanding General of the Marine Corps Recruit Depot has asked that I inform you that your new Marine has arrived at Parris Island. We have instructed him to write to you regularly. You will find his mailing address on the first page of the General Information sheet enclosed. He receives mail once daily. It usually takes about a week after he mails this letter for your response to reach him. Please do not be alarmed if his first letters to you report that he has not received yours. We find, during the first week after their arrival, recruits are so anxious to receive mail that they do not fully realize that only a few days have passed. I think you will understand this when you consider that our training days are 16 hours long, and so much happens so quickly that it is inevitable for a recruit to lose track of the days.

But this does point up the value all recruits place on receiving mail. Being very busy and under stresses of adjusting to military life, they cherish their contacts with home more than ever. During this period of adjustment, which can last one to three weeks, it is not unusual for some recruits to feel depressed, dejected, or incapable of meeting the challenges and requirements of their new situation. You can help your Marine most by writing encouraging and cheerful letters to him as frequently as you will.

I have discussed the mail situation extensively because I place great importance on seeing that recruit mail is delivered promptly and properly. I know how important it is to them. I want to assure you that your Marine's other individual needs--his health, food, spiritual welfare, and any individual or special training requirements--are looked after and supervised with the same meticulous care as his mail. His officers and drill instructors are charged with caring for every aspect of his life and training here at Parris Island, and they do their jobs well.

Our responsibility in the Recruit Training Regiment is to transform your young man and thousands like him from a civilian into a basically trained Marine, capable of accepting full responsibility for his present and future roles in our Corps, living and functioning effectively in close contact with other young Marines, and accepting the demands of unit discipline. In the process he must prove to himself, his comrades, and his officers and drill instructors that he is worthy of the respect and confidence which are part of our title and uniform. Barring organic physical problems over which neither he nor we have any control, he can meet all challenges and clear all hurdles if he really wants to. More than one million Marines before him have done so!

In the General Information sheet you will find our regulations governing visits to your Marine. I suggest that you limit your visiting to Graduation Day and the evening hours of the day before graduation, except when urgent matters arise which cannot wait. We have found over the years that Sunday and holiday visits during the course of training tend to distract a recruit's attention from his training responsibilities. However, in cases where illness or difficulties encountered by the recruit result in his remaining at Parris Island longer than the normal training period, Sunday visits can be most helpful for all concerned.

Boot camp letter

The
United States
Marine Corps

Certificate of Acceptance

This is to certify that MICHAEL RODDIE FRENCH
has successfully passed the required mental,
moral and physical examinations
and has been accepted for enlistment
in the United States Marine Corps.

The defense of our country and our freedoms
is the duty and privilege of every citizen.
The Marine Corps has a proud tradition of
outstanding service to our country in
peace and war. Voluntary enlistment in this
elite military organization is a clear
demonstration of the American qualities
of patriotism and loyalty.

SSgt James W Kennedy
Recruiter, United States Marine Corps

Presented this 14th *day*

of JUNE , 19 73

By the Officer in Charge,
Marine Corps Recruiting Station

ME-66-73

Certificate of Acceptance from Staff
Sergeant Kennedy, my recruiter

After being released from the hospital, they sent two
Marine Corps recruits from platoon #257 to escort me back

to the barracks. I did not know where to go or where anything was. I was disoriented. After arriving at the barn—that's what they called it—I had the privilege of meeting one of my new drill instructors, DI Sergeant Johnson.

I could hear him screaming from two blocks away from the barracks. I could hear garbage cans being slung against the wall. There were three levels, and we were on the second level when the two recruits brought me there to the doorway. I saw about five recruits doing pushups, another three doing jumping jacks, two more running in place real fast, holding their rifles straight out in front of them, which were M14s, and screaming to the top of their lungs, "*I'm a scumbag, sir!*"

The other recruits doing exercises were screaming out loud to the top of their voices, "*Kill, kill, kill!*"

Sergeant Johnson was running around like a psycho, bending down and screaming at each one of these people straight in their ears and their faces and kept telling them, "*Faster, faster, faster!*" He was running around to different bunks while all of this other stuff was going on, tearing the bunks apart, turning the footlockers over, and footlockers are where we kept all of our clothes and shaving equipment as well as our other equipment. Everything was a mess in there.

When he turned around and noticed the two recruits, he had sent for me, and his eyes pierced right through me. I could see the veins in his head pop out. He stood up and started marching right to me, at the same time calling the squad bay to attention. The rest of the people in Platoon #257 were from Virginia, and he noted that to me right in my ear, then looked me straight in the eyes about a half an inch from my nose, screaming, "*What kind of maggot are you?*" He then asked me where I was from.

I told him the Chicagoland area, Chicago, Illinois. That was the first time that I thought my eyes were going to be knocked out of my head when he slapped me on the left side of the head. He told me then to get down in the pushup position and start doing pushups. He said I must be punished because I'm a liar. He said that I was not from Chicago and that I was a cockroach liar and not to ever say that I was from Chicago again where he could hear me. He told me that I was from Florida because that's where all the queers were and that I looked like one. That was my first introduction to this maniac DI Sergeant Johnson.

As I have been writing this book, I have been remembering things in detail, and it's not that hard to remember them in detail because I also feel them in every form and fashion. I even think sometimes I smell things from that era. I've already had to stop quite a few times and take breaks, and not short breaks; I'm talking about a day or more from writing this book, and the reason is I start sweating, have rapid breathing, and my heart pounds very fast and heavily.

Picture of DI Sergeant Johnson (He is the sergeant on the left)

My psychiatrist, Dr. Small at the Nashville VA, explained to me that I have high anxiety, and what's happening to me is panic attacks, which almost feels like heart attacks. He and I both worked together with medications that had these episodes somewhat under control. But where I am right now in my life in Arizona, I do not have any medications whatsoever for anything physical or mental. I will explain why this is happening to me later on in this book. I have digital tape recordings and videos that will also support anything and everything that I say. But for right now, I will leave you with my testimony and some pictures of DI Sergeant Johnson, the gas chamber, and other things at Parris Island that I had to go through, not to mention the hand grenade pit. *And why in the world would these mean people who, in fact, beat you, abuse you, and cause you every pain they could get in a hand grenade pit and give me live hand grenades and try to teach me how to throw them?*

When I held the grenade to my chest in my left hand and put my right finger in the ring, I was to pull the pin and throw at command. I would be lying to all of you if I said that I did not think about picking up the whole box of grenades and throwing the live one in with them and jumping right on Sergeant Johnson as they all went off. There was like a haze, and everything just went still, and I couldn't hear anything as I was thinking these thoughts. At the age of seventeen, I do believe this is the first time in my life where I experienced anxiety, depression, sadness, madness, and fear at the same time in one bundle. The fear is the only thing that stopped me from doing it. Not fear of him, not fear of the Marine Corps, but fear of God. Because I felt him telling me at that instant that it was not the right thing to do. He was with me then, and he's with me now. He's with everybody that seeks him. So now let's get on with the testimony and pictures.

DI Sergeant Johnson

Assault Course Parris Island Picture

CLOSE COMBAT

Close Combat Parris Island Picture

Confidence Course Parris Island Pictures

Confidence Course Picture

Confidence Course Picture

Confidence Course Picture

Confidence Course Picture

Elliots Beach Picture

Elliots Beach Picture

Elliots Beach Picture

Firing Pistol Parris Island Picture

Testimony: Michael R. French, USMC Boot Camp, June to September 1973

On June 6, 1973, I entered boot camp at Parris Island for the USMC. Two or three weeks into boot camp, it was exposed that I have an allergy to penicillin. The allergic reaction caused me to be hospitalized a couple weeks where I was in a coma and took some time to recover.

Upon release from the hospital, I was reassigned to a new platoon, #257, with the main DI being Sergeant Johnson. DI Sergeant Johnson seemed to single me out as I was the only recruit from the Chicago area while he claimed to also be from the same area. The other recruits in Platoon #257 were all from Virginia.

Being singled out, DI Sergeant Johnson was very excessive in his daily harassment of me. Some incidents include hitting me with the stock of a rifle in the solar plexus and other body parts, hitting me in the head with my footlocker after commanding me to lay on the floor, and many other daily beatings. On one occasion, I was ordered to clean the head and went in with my bath shower shoes and skivvies. DI Sergeant Johnson claimed I was not doing it fast enough and started kicking me on various parts of my body. He ordered me to do push-ups in the head and proceeded to sodomize me in my rectum with a baton-like wooden object while I was prone in the push-up position.

This continued until DI Sergeant Johnson commanded me to return to squad bay and stand at attention. While only in my bath shoes and skivvies, other recruits were present and witnessed the blood that was on my boxers. On another occasion, I was commanded to stand at attention after chow and was distracted by a television broadcast or something that made me turn my head. DI Sergeant Johnson slapped me on the side of the head so hard, I saw stars. DI Sergeant Johnson then proceeded to order me to return to my bottom bunk where he commanded me to put both feet on the top steel bunk, put my head and arms on the concrete floor, and he made me pretend I was changing channels on the dials. I was kept in this position for an hour or more.

On another occasion, during a PT run, I overheated and got sick, which caused me to stop and throw up in mid-run. It was caused by the salt tabs added to our water canteens to prevent dehydration. DI Sergeant Johnson then kicked me repeatedly very hard in the stomach, stating he "wanted to be sure all of the salt tabs were gone so I could continue the run."

On yet another occasion, we were on the rifle range in the prone shooting position on our bellies. DI Sergeant Johnson came up behind me, put his foot in my crotch, and proceeded to step on my testicles. He did not move and stated, "If you miss one shot, you will never have babies again." On another occasion for training in gas mask usage or attacks, we were in the gas chamber and told to take a very deep breath before removing our masks. After removing the mask, we were to give our name, rank, and serial number.

Another training step that was required was for us to clear the mask of any gas and replace it on our heads for continued use. Before I could do this, DI Sergeant Johnson grabbed the mask from my hands and proceeded to put it over my head, backwards, choking me and forcing me to breath in the gas that was not cleared from the mask. The choking continued until I thought I was going to pass out. When the mask was removed, I was coughing and gagging and then pushed out the door where I continued to cough and gag for many minutes.

A nightly event from DI Sergeant Johnson was to approach my bunk after our bedtime prayer to "hope for war with China," and the DI claimed he did not hear my prayer. This resulted in blows to my stomach or other body parts and went on during all of my basic training with this DI. I was subjected to this and similar incidents for a total of ten to eleven weeks before graduation from the USMC Parris Island Boot Camp.

One or more other recruits pressed for an investigation and/or charges for these unorthodox abuses by DI Sergeant Johnson with myself and several others being ordered to stay at Parris Island to submit our testimony against him after graduation from boot camp.

Being forced to stay left me with extra KP duty while waiting for the trial/hearing. While on the extended stay in Parris Island and KP duty, I was repeatedly threatened by USMC personnel and/or recruits that if I testify against DI Sergeant Johnson, I would never leave Parris Island alive. During this time, I was also assaulted at my bunk with the bunk being flipped, hot water poured over me while sleeping, banging on doors and the steel bunk while sleeping, etc.

Being only seventeen years of age at the time, these actions left me scared to death. I contemplated suicide, disappearing into the swamps surrounding Parris Island, or finding any means possible to leave boot camp. I threw up chow regularly during these times due to the extreme stress, fear, and debasing caused by DI Sergeant Johnson.

In retrospect, these events have caused me to be rebellious and not trusting of any other human being outside of my immediate family for all of my adult years. I voluntarily joined the USMC to serve my country and be one of "the few, the proud, the Marines." I served out my term as a Marine, but the tremendous negative impact to my life caused by these situations continues to make me question if I made the right decision.

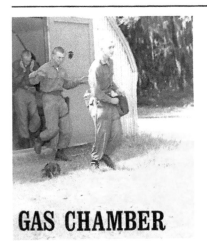 

Gas Chamber Parris Island Pictures

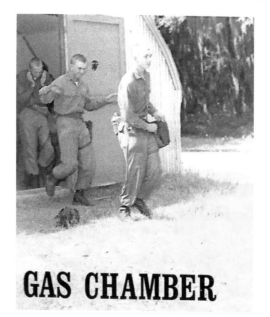

Gas Chamber Picture

Gas Chamber Picture

Gas Chamber Picture

Gas Chamber Picture

HAND GERNADES

Hand Grenades Parris Island picture

Infiltration Course Parris Island Picture

Infiltration Course Parris Island Picture

Infiltration Course Parris Island Picture

My Rifle Prayer Parris Island Picture

OBSTACLE COURSE

Obstacle Course Parris Island Picture

Parris Island Picture

PHYSICAL TRAINING

Physical Training Parris Island Picture

3

After the Court-Martial
of Sergeant Johnson

Still at Parris Island and graduating, I received the rank of Private First Class. It was the first time that I felt honored. It was like I could breathe again. I tried to bury all of the negative thoughts away. I was still shaky and scared but felt almost like a human being.

They gave me my first paycheck at Parris Island, and I had about a week before I could go on my thirty-day leave to see my parents. I felt proud that I got through all of this. So I went to the PX. I noticed a necklace with a tiny baby Marine Corps ring on it, so I bought it and sent it to my mother along with a satin scarf that had embroidery about Parris Island on it. I wanted her to know I was okay.

I couldn't call so much because back then, collect calls were very expensive. I still own and have the scarf and the ring to this day that was willed back to me by my mother. Some things in life you can never forget.

The day came when we were told and given orders of where to go for our next duty station in schooling and our thirty-day leave. I flew back to Chicago, and my parents picked me up at the O'Hare airport in Chicago. Things seemed like a dream. It was like I was there but not there.

I spent time with my parents, and my mom cooked meals for me. But the only thing I wanted to do was get into my car and drive up and down the streets, thinking about all of the things that happened to me and trying to forget most of them. No matter how hard I tried and how many other things I tried to think about, I just couldn't get this out of my mind: why would anybody say that they are part of a team with you, yet stomp you in the ground? I don't understand.

Even though I found out that Sergeant Johnson had just gotten back from Vietnam himself, he should have been debriefed and taught how to treat new innocent teenagers to properly go into war and defend our country. That's just my opinion, but I do believe that would be the most sensible way to teach someone. So was it just Sergeant Johnson? Or was that the standard back then? For me and several other people who were in boot camp with me, it did not work that way. If you want someone to be your ally in anything in life, you cannot mistreat them. You have to educate them. Would you do that to your own children?

My high school friends would talk to me, and they were laughing, smiling, and proud and happy to see me, but it was like I was not even there. I was so jumpy. I remember standing in line at a Dairy Queen. A high school buddy, Bill, came up behind me. My hands were in my pants pockets. He touched my elbow and said, "Hey" or something like that. I ripped my whole left pants pocket and leg of my pants because I jerked so hard when he touched me.

Michael French

You know they say they teach Marines to defend our country? That's the outside. On the inside, they want you to be killers, and I mean killers with no regret and no remorse. I wonder if any of them have loving families that are not raised in fear. Even then, the men, the Marines—in boot camp, mind you—were taught that a woman marine was to be called a "BAM," which means Broad Ass Marine. The naval personnel were "squids." They were weak and not as good as us. The army and air force all were treated with the same disrespect because we carried the emblem of the globe, anchor, and eagle—eagle meaning air, anchor meaning sea, and globe meaning land or the world.

Yes, I was proud of this, *but* these people also should be respected and given honor for defending our country and not ridiculed and disgraced and laughed at. That's how we make this a great country by all joining together. But the Marine Corps I was in did not teach this, especially in boot camp. And especially from Sergeant Johnson. I can still feel the blows to my stomach from not reciting at attention in my bunk with my rifle loud enough, "Pray for war in China."

48

4

Cherry Point, North Carolina
Heavy Equipment School
Still the Nightmares

Upon arriving at Cherry Point, I was introduced to Captain Bell. He was my commanding officer. I felt so alive with him. He was so encouraging and uplifting. It was in November, just before Thanksgiving in 1973, and I passed all of my driving courses with flying colors. I was so happy and was told—we were all told—we could take leave for Thanksgiving to see our families.

We took a week off to see our families, and then when I came back on my eighteenth birthday of December 6, I was going to take another thirty-day leave. I didn't understand at the time why there was so much leave. Captain Bell explained I've got orders, and since I was eighteen, I was going to be sent overseas in the far east because I was needed there.

So the nightmares came back, the words that Sergeant Johnson drilled into my head: *"Kill, kill, kill!"* It was snowing in Chicago when I arrived, and again, for thirty days,

I drove my car up and down the streets, trying to think, *What have I gotten myself into?* And those thirty days on leave were definitely filled with sleepless nights.

My parents brought me back to O'Hare, and this time, I would be gone for over a year. It was very saddening, but one thing I learned from Sergeant Johnson was that I should hold everything in.

5

Heading East

I flew out of Chicago to Los Angeles, and from there on a propjet to Anchorage, Alaska. We stopped on the runway and got out of the propjet and walked across the landing field to the terminal. The wind was so strong and it was so cold.

We got into the terminal, and at that time, I looked at the Coca-Cola machine, and it was one dollar for a coke or cold drink. On the mainland of the United States where I was from, it was only a quarter. Alaska was a dollar. We stayed there for quite a while until the early morning, waiting for the sun to come out because the plane was frozen. Then we embarked from Anchorage to Iwakuni, Japan, where we were told to remain in the propjet we had to refuel.

We started our descent after a couple of hours to Okinawa. We were supposed to be back up for Cambodia evacuation, but we were to regroup at Okinawa. Upon arriving at Okinawa, I could see this tiny island. It was approximately seventy miles long and thirty-five miles wide. But with all of the mountain ranges and caverns and caves, that tiny island held so many people, military and Japanese civilians.

My orders were to report to Camp Hansen Gate Two, Seventh Communication Division. When I got off of the plane at Kadena Airforce Base, I remembered Sergeant Johnson and how he put down the air force, but I realized everything he told me was a lie because they were definitely our allies. But don't get me wrong because when I was stationed at Cherry Point driving school that was also known as Cherry Point Marine Corps Air Station, we were with some incredible fighting planes like you never saw before. That also made me very, very proud.

I'm sorry about my flashbacks. Some of my flashbacks are okay, but most of them rip my guts out, so let me get back to my journey to the base.

We were transported in what they called a cattle car, and that is exactly what it looked like, like something cattle would ride in, to Camp Hansen in the village of Kinlo. I went to gate two and reported into the Seventh Communication Division of the United States Marine Corps. But while driving from Kadena to Camp Hansen, I was looking out the window, and it was phenomenal but really strange at the same time. I did not understand any of the words on the buildings.

I found out that the Japanese alphabet has about five hundred and some odd characters and is written upside down and backwards, where ours only has twenty-six letters to the alphabet. This was all thrilling to me, and it uplifted me. Even in the back of my mind, I knew the war was still going on and what I might have to face. But much to my surprise, upon arriving in Seventh Communication Division, I met my great commander, Captain Darby, and then Staff Sergeant Ederalin. I was working as their company driver. Right away, I got promoted to Lance Corporal. Then I was told if I extended to seventeen months overseas duty that they would put me in for Corporal; that is considered NCO or Non-Commissioned Officer.

During the first few months of 1974, we were going to embark to Cambodia and the Kangaroo Two operation to pull some of the Vietnamese out and bring them to America. This lasted about two months, and it was back to Okinawa.

I wanted to extend again and stay in Okinawa, but then I found out the Geneva Convention was to be signed in 1975 and the war would be over. I had to come back to the States, then to Camp Lejeune, North Carolina. Once again, I had to leave some good people behind.

6

The Devil Dogs Bite Again
Camp Lejeune

After the thirty-day leave from Okinawa to see my parents, I proceeded to Camp Lejeune, North Carolina, and checked in at the second marine truck battalion. This was really different. Since I was a corporal/NCO at the time, which means Non-Commissioned Officer, there was more responsibility on my plate. Everyone got along as we always did in the motor pool. Then a hardcore commanding officer from recon transferred to be in charge of the motor pool. His name was Captain Sink. He supposedly had a steel plate in the left side of his head. I did see the scars all over his bald head and two sets of eyes: one with the Marine Corps emblem in the eye that he wore daily, and one with a skull and crossbones.

The skull and crossbones he would wear only when he was upset or giving office hours, and that means like a little court in his office or court-martials down at the battalion headquarters. Needless to say, he wore the skull and crossbones most of the time. One night, me and another marine buddy went to town in Jacksonville, North Carolina. This town was right outside the base. We got something to eat and walked around. Then we headed back to my car. As I was backing out, I bumped another car. An officer came, and we exchanged insurance cards. That's what my insurance agent of State Farm insurance explained for me to do if there was ever an accident.

When Captain Sink found out about it, he made a big deal because I didn't come and tell him, and I told him that I gave the girl my insurance through the police officer. Everything was passed back and forth, tag numbers and everything and names. But that was not enough for Captain Sink. This guy was about six-foot-four and acting like a wild man. You could only imagine how I felt after I witnessed his rage, and he told me that he was going to court-martial me. It was like Sergeant Johnson again in boot camp but in a different way.

On the day of the court-martial, Battalion Headquarters Second Marine Division, he was outraged, screaming to the top of his voice, talking about how I was a no-good person and not a marine and all kinds of bad things. I couldn't believe it. So I ended up losing a stripe and was busted down to Lance Corporal.

That night and weeks after, I couldn't sleep. I kept having flashbacks over and over again. You see, I was very proud after boot camp to go up in my ranks so fast. Now when something like this happens, they transfer the person who has been in trouble to a different area. I was transferred to Navy Dental to be their driver on the base of Camp Lejeune. That lasted for about three or four months. Then I was transferred out to the Second Truck Battalion where I got in trouble. I was really nervous when I was reporting to my new job assignment. But I found out Captain Sink was no longer there or even most of the troops I knew. I don't know where they sent him or where he got orders to, but I was so glad he was gone.

7

Deja Vu

Upon checking in with my commanding officer, I could not believe what he told me I saw and witnessed. He knew everything about me from boot camp onward, and he held it against me, I'm sure. I know what he told my mom and dad when they came to visit me in the brig which he put me in. Oh, by the way, his name was Major Johnson, like Sergeant Johnson in boot camp in the first part of my book. But let me tell you what happened before the ninety-day brig time.

This guy, Major Johnson, was only about five-foot-one, maybe at the most. He also had his face burned I guess from Vietnam. He was muscular on the top part of his little body and as mean as a snake. Everyone was afraid of him also. These are the type of people that are really nice to you in wartime when you have grenades and loaded rifles, but here in the States, we would only go to the armory and check weapons out to requalify. That was maybe once every year. He's another guy that brought back a lot of memories.

Finally, a sergeant friend of mine came and spoke with me. He said he had to get out of there for a while and if I wanted to go? When I asked him what he meant, he said, "Let's take your car. I will pay for gas. Let's go on a short vacation for a couple of days. They will never miss us."

I was really tired of all this happening over and over again. The commanding officers were reflecting on my boot camp records. It was so bad I had to leave. I couldn't stand it anymore. So we traveled down to Walt Disney World in Florida, then Daytona beach. I even laid back in the sand on the beach and started to fall asleep, only to be woken up from a nightmare.

We headed back to Camp Lejeune. We both dreaded going back. In fact, they did miss us, and we were in big trouble. They charged both of us with UA, which means Unauthorized Absence. But getting to the point, there was another court martial, and I lost two more stripes then, which meant that I was private starting all over again.

My mom and dad came down to the brig that I was in to see me for a short while and to pick up my car and tow it back home. But while they were there, Major Johnson was there also. He told my parents that I was no good to their faces and in front of me. I can't remember everything, but it was all bad, and he would not even let my mother give me a hug or even let my mom or dad touch me at all. He claimed that was the rule, but I don't believe it.

I was supposed to have gotten ninety days in brig, but I did in fact get out in seventy-five days for good behavior. Once again, I reported back to the Second Truck Battalion, and once again, I did not see anybody I knew. We were spray-painting jeeps—olive drab, of course—and all of a sudden, my chest started beating like fifty times faster than normal and harder. They called the core man medical team to come down. They laid me in the back of a truck, then brought me to the hospital.

They said that it was beating so fast they could not get a count. They gave me some kind of a shot in my arm. It took about an hour before my heart slowed down. I don't know what caused this unless it was the spray paint that we were using on the jeeps. It was never talked about again, like my coma in boot camp from penicillin. Everything was just pushed under the rug and forgotten. So it was close to my discharge date, and a nice man that was a lieutenant colonel let me out with an honorable discharge three months earlier than I was supposed to get out because I did some extra work for him.

8

Free at Last
Illinois Bound

I felt so alive when that jet touched down in Chicago. I told the taxi to go straight to my mom's address in Romeoville, Illinois. They paid me my last check when I got out of the Marine Corps before I left Camp Lejeune, four hundred and twenty some odd dollars.

Of course, the family was glad to see me again. First job I got was as a security guard at Western Electric. It was third shift from 11:00 p.m. to 7:00 a.m. Then I got a part-time side job from about nine to three roofing houses. I only wanted to start succeeding in life and to put everything behind me. But the big green monster had to come one more time. What I mean is I went to eat at my mom's house one evening about 4:00 p.m. after roofing. Then I got a call from Camp Lejeune. They claimed that I owed them money. They said about four hundred and twenty-two dollars.

My last check that was given to me approximately a week before my discharge. Because they do not pay you ahead of time, they pay you after the month is over what you have done. So actually, they owed me a week's more pay, but I couldn't explain this to the guy on the phone because he wouldn't listen. He told me that if I didn't pay the money back to the address he gave me that I would never be in good standing with the Marine Corps. I laughed at him and said I didn't care because since day one of boot camp, they made it clear to me and several others that we were not in good standing with the Marine Corps, that we were only dirt bags.

All of this stuff still plays over and over in my head and still does. This is my first time speaking publicly about these situations, except for a few choice doctors, my mother and Stephanie, and a few close other sorts that I won't mention at this time. Oh, and by the way, in my opinion, all doctors should not be considered doctors or called doctors, especially the ones that are supposed to listen to you when you have an emotional problem such as mine. They just sit back and look at you, and at last, they state there is a group I could go to outside of the VA hospital to talk to who had the same problems that I did. What does this doctor think about something so terrifying that you have to carry around all of your life? How can he even think that I can go to a group of people that I don't even know and start talking about my past? And what is he paid for anyway?

This particular doctor will be in the latter part of my book where I am going to include tape recordings and video tapes. I learned how to use this spy equipment because these type of individuals, nine times out of ten, will swear on the Bible that they never said this or that or don't remember. I think it is only justified and fair that myself and others in this world that have been wrongfully done should help these people, like my doctors, with a video tape/tape recording and don't forget to put down a preamble before you start recording, which means the date, time, month, and year and the person's name whom you are talking to. This is called a one-party consent law, which means you can have a tape recorder on your person, speak to someone, and record the whole conversation, and it is perfectly legal. It is a federal and state statute. Not all states will go along with this law, so you have to be careful so that you don't get into trouble.

Okay, back to living in Illinois. I'm free, I'm out, I have to try to forget about this mess. I find it very hard keeping employment because of a lack of sleep. Also, relationships with females never last. Sometimes I would turn to alcohol so I could pass out at night. But then I would feel terrible the next day. Not to mention the dreams, the flashbacks, and the horror that goes with it. I keep having a dream waking up in boot camp and finding out I signed up for four more years. Seems like the same thing over and over.

I had to try something different in life. I knew how to play the guitar from when I was ten years old, so I put together some chords and some lyrics and recorded two 45 records. They played on the local radio stations around the Chicagoland area and were requested by listeners to be played again. But that wasn't paying the bills very much. I tried several other jobs. When bosses, supervisors, foremen, etc., were demanding with me, raising their voices, all I could see was Sergeant Johnson's face, especially when one or two had the guts to belittle me in front of other people.

I remember at this time in my life I had not sought mental help for this problem. You might call it embarrassment, shame, humiliation in the highest form of what DI Sergeant Johnson did to me. So I just kept it all in, which resulted in more drinking of alcohol and fights, and both of them resulted in jail time most of the time. I was trying to find a way to escape from the memories that had haunted me, but they always would come back. So I decided to get away again.

This time I chose to go to Tennessee where I could pursue music. I found a place about eighty miles from Nashville where I was teaching music in a small music store and working with my landlord slaughtering hogs to pay the rent. Plus, he would give me sausage, pork chops, different meats from the pig, which helped out a lot. I struggled playing music and doing other odd jobs for quite some time. It was pretty rough, so in 1986, my mother sold her house and moved to Tennessee and bought another home so she could retire. The cost of living and taxes were cheaper there.

I went to visit my mom around that time, 1987 or so. The lower part of my stomach was cramping and hurting so bad. Also, there was blood coming out in my stool. Finally, I started getting dizzy, so Mom got a hold of the county human resources, and they paid for me to go to a doctor in Jackson, Tennessee. His name was Dr. Sauder. He did an endoscopy and colonoscopy on me. He did not know anything of my past in the Marine Corps because I did not want him to do the proceedings from the rectum up. All kinds of things were going through my mind about the past and everything.

He saw that I was nervous about it but did not know why exactly. He reassured me that everything would be all right and that most definitely, I needed the procedure because there could be something terribly wrong to cause the bleeding and the pain. After two nights of enemas and laxatives, etc., they came into my room and started an IV of anesthesia, and the next thing I knew, they were bringing me back to my room. He told me that they took nine cancerous polyps out of me, and he would call my mom's home in a few days after the biopsies.

My mom and I wondered how I could have ended up like that. The wonder was a great shock when I found out that the Marine Corps had another hand in this, which will be revealed in the latter part of my book. But good news was coming from Dr. Sauder. The polyps were not malignant. He said I would be okay for the time but to keep checking on this periodically.

About 1990, I made my mind up to go back to Chicagoland area and find a better job and just do music on the side. So I found a job installing cable. That lasted until 1998. I was involved in an accident on the job, which led me to some time off, so I started writing songs again.

I met Gary Loizzo, the owner of Pumpkin Recording Studios and the producer of many top artists. He chose to be my mentor and recorded my music with also he himself singing backup on some of my material and co-writing a few of my songs, which are copywritten at the Library of Congress, Washington DC. I was told that a lot of my songs sounded depressing, but in a good way. Then some-body even said that I should name my CD "The Man with the Broken Heart." But I kept trying to play music and doing more odd jobs. I just could not shake the feeling, anxiety, and depression away from me, and the nightmares persisted.

I was worried about my mom being alone. Yet, I knew that I was going to find out, down the road, what was really wrong with me and where it came from. I knew in the back of my mind what was going on with me. I just kept trying to suppress all of the thoughts and feelings. Like I said, I knew I was going to find out. So I continued with music up in Illinois and then in Long Island, New York, and back and forth, but I would go back every weekend to take care of my mom and buy her supplies. She was the only one I could talk to who actually knew what had happened to me in boot camp, besides the officers that held the investiga-tion and the other men in my platoon that witnessed the abuse and who also suffered abuse themselves.

Around the year of 2002, I made my mind up to go and be with my mom continuously. She had a bad heart, rheumatoid arthritis, and ten ruptures in her stomach, which the doctors sewed in a mesh that did not hold. She also had degenerated disc disease. She needed someone, so it was my responsibility. I made it my responsibility. She was my mother but also my best friend.

I remember when I was working in Chicago in 1994, I found an old Bible with no back, no cover on it, but it had large letters, so I reconditioned the Bible and brought it to her in Tennessee so she would be able to read it. We used to call one another once a week and study over the phone.

Until about the date of April 1995, when she called me, she sounded so desperate, so sincere. She said she wanted to be baptized as soon as possible. She got baptized on April 10, 1995, at the Church of Christ in Lockport, Illinois. Earlier, I had gotten baptized at the Church of Christ in Nashville, Tennessee, in 1991. I brought her back home to Tennessee and pursued my music and everything until 2002. I had saved enough money then for about two years to support myself and my mom with food and what not. Her house was already paid for, the taxes was very low, and the utilities were very cheap.

So I went back to Tennessee. She wouldn't have to pay for anyone to mow her lawn because I was there. I was there to bring her to the doctors and to cook and clean for her. I was just returning the kindness that she gave me from my childhood and all my life. In my opinion, this is what any child should do for a parent. There was no way I was going to throw her into an old folks' home.

Mom also had been diagnosed with edema. She used to retain quite a bit of fluid in her legs and ankles, so she had to lie down a lot after she took her medication. That way, some of the water could pass. About three or four in the afternoon, she used to wake up and come outside with me in the screened-in sunroom and talk about different things. My money was running low, so I started selling my musical equipment. I had about thirty thousand dollars worth of top-notch equipment that I had bought in Chicago before I left. So in 2006, I sold my last Gibson gold-plated jumbo acoustic electric guitar. You can imagine I did not get what I spent for it. Those things are only material anyway.

I told Mom I was thinking about going and getting some odd jobs, but she had noticed that I was nervous and shaky all the time, more now than in the beginning because when she was sleeping during the daytime, I would sit in the sunroom and do a lot of thinking about my past. It just got worse and worse.

She wanted me to file for disability, but I felt ashamed. After all, I was only fifty-two at that time. About 2003 to 2006, I did a lot of checking and talked with a lot of people who were on disability for different reasons. I made my mind up to go to the state doctors, one for Social Security and one at the DAV in Nashville. They both put me through a battery of tests, physical and mental. I got an attorney to handle the social security, and an attorney advocate at the Nashville DAV.

The social security attorney was dragging his feet, so I decided to call Nashville, Tennessee, and the deciding judge in the disability office. His secretary spoke with me, very concerned. She told me to send all of my doctors' reports and everything pertaining to my case. She also said to call her back within one week. When I called her back, she told me she was sending out the letter that was fully approved 100 percent disabled, but it would be a while before I received any compensation.

I formally filed in 2007 with the DAV and started receiving one thousand dollars a month in pension, but I could not receive 100 percent disability until it was known that it was service connected. So I started seeing the VA psychiatrist, dental, foot doctors, back doctors, and everything to get myself straightened out. It was very hard at that point in life, even though a little money was coming in. It was hard, mentally and physically, for me and my mother.

Mom would ride along with me to my VA appointments. The main reason is because I did not want to leave her alone. I would push her in the wheelchair to my appointments. But one day, going to the parking lot to the car at the VA hospital, my mother threw up all in the front floorboard. I cleaned her up and tried to get her to go in the hospital. She refused and said she was okay. It looked like coffee grounds that came out.

When we got back to our home, her house, I helped her inside of the sunroom and sat her down on the swing. She threw up again but this time acted like she was going to pass out. I called the emergency. A police officer came as we were waiting for the ambulance and saw the coffee ground-like vomit and said it was blood. She had to be rushed to the Paris, Tennessee, hospital which was about eighteen miles away. Camden Hospital was not much of a hospital. They couldn't handle too many fatal incidents. She had to have four transfusions of blood.

Well, we finally got through that, and she was back home in about a week. This was in 2007. Mom and I both ended up with the flu about Christmas time of 2007. We contracted the flu virus at a clinic in Paris, Tennessee, where a lady was looking right at us and coughing right on us without covering her mouth or anything. She was standing up as we were sitting down. That was early in the day. Late that night, my mother and I were both sick and throwing up and could not keep anything down. Just as we thought we were getting better, we would get worse.

This lasted until mid-January of 2008. Around February of 2008, we seemed to be okay. So in good spirits, Mom went with me to the Nashville VA again. I went to get all of my teeth removed. Some of them were getting really bad, and I didn't understand why. I didn't know it was going to be from the Marine Corps again why my teeth were falling out.

They said they could not do the full operation because I was not service connected, so I had to live with the pain. We lived our lives as happily as we could and talked about positive things. We had a good Thanksgiving in that year of 2008, just Mom and myself. She came with me to another VA appointment in December just before Christmas. I had to bring another man with a driver's license with us to the appointment. They said I needed a driver after the surgery.

They took all of my teeth out that day and sent me home with dentures. They would have to be refitted when the swelling went down. There was only one big problem that day. There was a lot of sick people at that hospital. My mother and myself both contracted the flu virus again. So all through Christmas, January, and February, we were fighting the flu again. I made sure we had every kind of medicine that was ever made at the house. Then the beginning of March 2009 came around, and we seemed to be a lot better.

Then a funny thing happened. A woman called about seven o'clock one evening in the beginning of March and said to my mother over the phone, "When you die, who do I contact to get my share?"

I thought this was very odd, and it made my mother cry because this woman chose not to see my mom in eighteen years and only called her once a year on the phone. And by the way, she was only four hundred miles away from my mom. That's all I have to say about that in this book. This book is titled *Honorably Dishonored*, and I felt my mom in my heart being very much dishonored that night.

Around April 5, on Mom's birthday, she started getting weak. I brought her to the doctor in Paris, Tennessee. The doctor said her oxygen level was eighty-eight. I did not know at that time that she was supposed to have been hospitalized if the oxygen level was that low. So I brought her back home as instructed by the doctor. The doctor also told me that if there were any change for the worse to bring her back. Well, there was a bad change the very next day. The doctor in Paris was about twenty miles away.

I was trying to get Mom to the car. She was collapsing in my arms. I used all the strength I had to get her in the car safely, but I did not bring her to Paris. I brought her to the Camden Tennessee ER. I ran inside and got the doctors. They, in turn, airlifted my mother to the Jackson Tennessee General Hospital.

I went home to get my recorders and swiftly proceeded to Jackson General Hospital. After being detained for about two hours, I demanded to see my mother to find out her condition. After seeing her, she had oxygen hooked up to her and IVs, and she still had a smile on her face.

The doctor said she had pneumonia and that the doctor in Paris should have never let her go home. The doctor told me that he was going to airlift her to Nashville, Tennessee, to Saint Thomas Hospital because her condition was very serious. I had already driven sixty miles west to Jackson from Camden. Now I had to drive east to Nashville another one hundred and fifty miles. I'm not complaining, but why couldn't Camden have sent her to Saint Thomas in the first place?

Then I proceeded to drive to Nashville Saint Thomas, and when I got there, they had her already hooked up on the oxygen machine. I had to sign papers because I had power of attorney. They put a breathing tube down her throat and wanted to induce her into a coma. After they explained the reasoning, I went ahead and signed for that. They said it was common practice on patients like this. So I drove back home that night with an assurance that she would be okay. I came back to mom's house, prayed, and then went to sleep.

I got up the next day, and called the hospital to check on her. Her status was the same. I checked the mail and found out from a letter that the Marine Corps was not finished torturing me. The letter told me to call the commandant of the Marine Corps in North Carolina. They said that I was exposed to toxic water poisoning from Camp Lejeune. They said the wells were contaminated from 1957 to 1987 with TCE, PCE, vinyl chloride, benzene, and dry-cleaning fluid. They wanted me to register, which I did. They said anybody that was there in that period for thirty days or more would be contaminated. I was there

for two years until March of 1977. This probably explains
the rapid heartbeat and the cancerous polyps in my colon.
This is what they told me, but I was to know there was
more damage to come to my body from this toxic water
poisoning.

I continued visiting Mom about four times a week. I
went down there the second week, and some doctor wanted
to talk to me about a biopsy. He called me out in the hallway and sat down with me and asked me if I would sign
for them to take a biopsy of Mom's lungs. I asked him what
good it would do. He said, "It might let us know how to
treat someone else in this condition."

I asked him how it would affect my mother.

He told me then it would be a fifty-fifty percent chance
that she would live or die with this proceeding.

My blood started to boil. I can't even tell you the
words that came out of my mouth toward that jerk, and
he knew never to cross my path again after that one time.
A power of attorney is very much essential for a loved one.
Otherwise, they can do just about anything they want to
do if there is no one with authority to stand guard. Always
remember this. I talked with the doctor because her tongue
was swelling out of her mouth with the feeding tube in it,
and it was dried and cracked. Her body looked like it was
swollen three times its original size. So I decided to sign for
a tracheotomy and a feeding tube which would not only
give her nutrition but be a diuretic for her to get the water
off of her body.

A week after that, her oxygen level was at 42 percent. With my anxiety level at an all-time high from what

happened to me at boot camp, the toxic water in North Carolina, and Mom with this, I didn't know how I was going to hold on. I just had to keep busy and didn't want anyone around me. But then I get a phone call from Sylvia, only to make things worse. Just before Mom got out of the hospital, I was talking to Sylvia over the phone one night and crying about Mom and worried about Mom, and I told her that I didn't know what I would do if anything ever happened to my mom. Sylvia was supposed to have been my mom's best friend, even though they didn't see each other in person. They were just like phone friends.

Sylvia then told me as I was crying that she knew how I felt and if I wanted to go ahead and commit suicide if anything happened to my mom, it would be okay. I just froze because after that she told me that if my mom died, she knew the house would be in my name through the will and it was okay for me to commit suicide but to first go down to Judge Whitworth's office, who was also an attorney in town, and legally sign mom's house over to her. Judge Whitworth is the one who made the will for my mother, and Sylvia already knew this. She knew that the house and all of my mother's possessions would be solely in my name, including the bills. I was the only one responsible for everything. Then I could commit suicide.

I froze then and told her to hold on for a second. I went to get my microcassette tape recorder. Also, I had another tape recorder hooked up directly in line through our phone system in the house, which meant any phone I lifted up or answered, the tape recording would start taping. After about two or three minutes, I had the recorders wired and ready to go. I went back to the sunroom and picked up the handheld phone and told Sylvia, "Sorry, I had to go do something real fast." I asked her to please repeat the instructions to me of what she previously told me. When I was sure I got everything recorded with the date and time of her telling me to commit suicide if my mom passed away and signing everything over to her, I quickly made an excuse to get off the phone with this ugly person.

One week after Mom got out of the hospital and was home with me, Mom had the chance to hear the truth about this ugly, ugly person. Mom called her right away and acted as usual and led her into the conversation of what she told me. After Sylvia tried to lie and weasel her way out of what was said to me, Mom played her the tape recording and told her never to call her number again.

Mother's Day in 2009, I came to visit my mother, and they were bringing her out of her induced coma for a short time so she could speak with me. She was so out of it that she couldn't recognize me or even know what she was saying. Her oxygen level then at that point was about sixty-seven, so I knew she was getting better. I left flowers and a Mother's Day card and some other gifts in case she woke up so she could see them, and then I drove back eighty-eight more miles back home. I wanted to fix the place up for her for when she got back, so I had the entire house painted, white Berber carpet installed, a new sink and faucet in the kitchen, a new vanity in the bathroom and toilet, laid new tile down in the kitchen, dining room, and bathroom, a new stove hood, new sheets and comforter for her bed, new robes, and dusters like a zip-up daytime gown for her. I also tiled the cabinet tops in the kitchen myself with a mosaic style.

I know these are all material things, but I had to keep myself busy. I wanted her to be happy when she came home. The time went past to the day that she said she was well enough to leave the hospital and go into a thirty-day rehab. This was toward the end of May. They brought her to some rehab close by the hospital there in Nashville. I walked up to see her in her room. They had her sitting up in some type of mechanical chair in her own feces. Her bed had feces all in it. They had plenty of staff standing around and laughing and talking right outside her door.

Mom could talk to me then. The trachea tube was removed. She still had her feeding tube though. She could not get up by herself or anything. At that point, her oxygen level was about eighty something. I asked her how long she had been sitting like this, and she said for a couple of hours and that her bottom was on fire from sitting in her own feces. I rushed out and asked people how come they hadn't taken care of her. They said they would get on it right away. I pretended that I was going to leave by telling them that I had a long drive back home, so I walked downstairs for about twenty minutes. The time then was about 4:30 p.m.

When I headed back up to her room, they had not done one thing for my mother, and she was sitting there, crying. I told her, "Don't worry, I will handle this." So I went straight downstairs to the coordinator's office, made my complaint, explained to them that I was going to the welfare people, and I wanted her out of this rehab right then and there.

I'll disclose the names, hospitals, people, etc., later in one of my other books, only because I have tape recordings, videos of the people, and places I am going to be speaking about in my book. Now, Dr. Thomas explained to me from Saint Thomas Hospital that Mom was only to go to rehab for thirty days and that their job was to exercise her and feed her proper nutrition to get her oxygen level well above ninety. So the next day, she was shipped to another rehab. When I went to her rehab facility in Nashville also, several doctors, people, and an attorney with the hospital and director wanted to meet with me. So we met in this big room with a long table. She had her own insurance to pay for anything and everything to be done. But what I didn't realize was this was not only a rehab, it was also a convalescent home for the elderly, and I only realized this during the meeting and what was being said to me.

The first thing they asked me was not concerning my mother's health or what they intended to do to make her get better, but what they did want to know and were very concerned about was how much she was receiving each month from social security. I knew right then I was right for having my recorder, recording the conversations and everything that was being said. But when they asked me that question, I told them that had nothing to do with the reason of why she was in here. I asked why they wanted to know this.

They said if she had to stay past thirty days, she would be considered living there in a convalescent home. Here again, my blood boiled. They said they were going to give her Ambien, which is a sedative that stopped her from being alert, and Dr. Thomas from Saint Thomas Hospital told me that she needed to be awake, alert, and gain energy and balance before she could be released. Her oxygen level needed to be well above ninety.

Then I told that board of scammers that I met with what the doctor said and told them I expected to have her exercised with small weights, like the doctor said, and ready to leave there within thirty days, and she would not have any Ambien or any kind of narcotics or opioids given to her, and I meant what I said. Then I pulled the tape recorder out of my jacket pocket and placed it in front of me where they all could see it. I started asking for all of their names. They all one by one started to get up and leave. I knew then I was dealing with some type of evil people trying to rape all of the older people of all of their funding from social security.

Mom finally got strong enough where she could call me at home from her room. They had a porta potty beside her bed, but she still needed help at that point. She called me one night and said she kept ringing for the nurse to come and she needed help to get to the potty. I told her to hang up, and I would call her right back. I had to call the nurse's station and make a complaint. I called her back and told her to stay on the phone with me until they came. It was about fifteen minutes, and then they finally came. I told Mom to call me when she was finished and back in bed.

It was about nine thirty at night now. I waited until ten thirty and had no call. When I tried to ring the nurse's station at the front desk, it would keep ringing, no answer.

This went on for about fifteen minutes. I then called the Nashville Tennessee Police Department precinct off of White Bridge road and explained the situation. I asked them if they would please do a welfare check on my mother.

I found out my mother was on the potty chair, teary-eyed and not being taken care of. They were really nice and said to call them back if I had any more problems or questions. My mother shortly called me after that. This type of thing kept going on an everyday basis. I tried to call the director of the hospital or even physically speak with her when I came down there, but they were nowhere to be found by phone or in person when they knew it was me that was looking or calling. I somehow knew this was going to happen. After that, I refused to sign any papers concerning Mom's disability income, which should not pertain to these people at all. Medicaid and Medicare took care of this. I had spoken with Dr. Thomas. He said she was well enough to come home. She just had to have her feeding tube taken out.

9

Finally, Mom Comes Home

It's June 30, 2009. I'm tossing and turning with dreams and cold sweats. I woke up about 4:00 a.m., not really sleeping, July 1, 2009, so I decided to stay up and have some coffee. I remember bits and pieces of my dreams, the yelling, the screaming at Parris Island boot camp. Right now, some people might think some of the things that were pounded in our brains were ridiculous and funny, like not killing a sand flea or mosquito because they were Marine Corps property, and we would be punished for it severely. I had to stay up all night long one time with no sleep to bury a mosquito that the DI Sergeant Johnson claimed that he saw me kill. I had to dig a two-by-four approximately four-foot deep grave for the mosquito that I never saw or don't remember swatting.

He came out and looked at the grave and said it was in the wrong place. He told me to cover that grave up, and approximately four feet away, he told me to dig another grave, the same two-by-four and four feet deep. When I completed that, he asked me where the mosquito was. I told him I didn't know where any mosquitos were and that

I didn't remember swatting any. He said to cover that grave up, then told me I must have dropped it in the first grave and to dig up the first grave over.

When I dug that grave back out, he measured to make sure it was two-by-four and four feet deep and told me to get in and find the dead Marine Corps mosquito. When I told him I could not find it, he started slapping me in the head, screaming and yelling, and told me to fill the grave back up. After I finished filling the grave up, I was dirty and sweaty, and mosquitos were swarming me, but I didn't dare slap at them at all. He made me start doing exercises. He said to do each exercise until he was tired.

Okay, enough of this right now. I'm talking about me picking up my mom. It was the first of July 2009, approximately 7:30 a.m. I was awake and had enough coffee. I didn't eat anything because after a night of dreams and sweats like that, I get sick to my stomach if I don't give myself enough time to calm down, which is usually a whole day. But that's okay. I had something to look forward to.

I was picking my mother up in Nashville from Saint Thomas Hospital. She was supposed to be brought from the rehab and to the hospital and arrive at 9:00 a.m. I remember I parked my car right at 9:00 a.m. As soon as I entered the hospital and walked down the hall where she was supposed to be, I saw her in a hospital bed being pushed by two male nurses, and she yelled out, "There he is!" She was talking about me. I guess she had told the male nurses that I was coming for her.

They stopped so I could have a word with her, and I gave her a kiss. We were both so happy. It only took about thirty seconds for the doctor to remove the feeding tube. He just pulled it out and put a Band-Aid on it. It was like a rubber straw. I asked, "Doesn't she need any stitches or anything?"

He said, "No, it will heal itself."

I asked him if she could walk or stand up, and he said yes. I brought new loose clothing for her that she could just slip over. I guess she called them muumuus or dusters. I went to get my car to bring to the front door. They said they had to bring her out in a wheelchair. It was hospital policy. Plus, she was too weak to walk a very long distance anyway. You figure she was in the hospital from mid-April, and now to the first of July on her back. Those rehabs did not exercise her like they were supposed to, like short walks up and down the hall—none of that was done. So we proceeded to drive back to Camden 87.6 miles.

When arriving in Camden, she had a taste for McDonald's, probably the only real food she had after all that time. When we pulled up in the driveway, I came around to help her in after unlocking all the doors in the house. I had to help her in and up the stairs. I asked her to close her eyes. I wanted to surprise her with all of the new things I did to the house. I helped her to the bathroom where I had set up a porta potty, which was higher than the toilet. I put it over the toilet. This way, she could brace herself and not have to sit all the way down. When she was finished, I walked her around all of her house and showed her all of the new things. She told me then that I was going to make it too pretty and we were not going to want to sell it then. Our plan was to sell that house and buy another one back up north or out west in Arizona.

We ate that night and watched some movies and drank iced water, just like old times. She seemed to be getting along pretty good. I had to bring her to the Paris, Tennessee, doctor the following week on the sixth, which was a Monday. Everything was looking up, except Mom was very disappointed with the doctor. The doctor was a woman that I won't mention this time until my other book, but that's the time that my mother was dishonored, and so were my feelings because they said they were going to stop giving her one of the daily medications that she needed with nitroglycerin already added into the prescription. She needed this medication badly.

The doctor said Medicaid and Medicare would not pay for that anymore and told my mother that if she had any heart spasms to just to take one of the regular nitro-glycerin tablets under her tongue and she should be okay.

My bedroom was right next to my mom's bedroom. I gave her a bell to ring. When she had to get up, she would ring it, and I would come to her aid and walk her safely to the bathroom or anywhere she needed to go, then escort her back to the bed. I did not want her to slip and fall anywhere. The doctor said her oxygen level was approximately ninety-three, the same doctor that sent her home when she had pneumonia when her oxygen level was in the eighties.

On the way home, I stopped and got a pizza at this one place we knew about. They made thin and crispy Chicago-style cut in squares the way she liked it. We got home, ate pizza, I cleaned up, brought her to her chair in the living room, we watched movies, and enjoyed the rest of the evening until bedtime. The rest of that week and weekend, I mowed the lawn and took care of chores that needed to be taken care of, at the same time keeping an eye on Mom.

On the thirteenth of July, I had an appointment with Chrysler in Paris, Tennessee, to drop my car off for warranty work to be done and to pick up a loaner car. I didn't want to leave Mom alone. I asked her if she was well enough and if she felt like riding with me. It was only about a half an hour there and half an hour back. I helped Mom into the loaner car and filled out paperwork for my warranty work to be done. Then we left to go back to Camden.

I stopped at Walmart on the way because I remember the doctor said humidity and moisture caused pneumonia besides the flu. So I bought a dehumidifier. This was Monday, the thirteenth of July 2009. I loaded it in the car. In between Walmart and Mom's house was a barbeque place that I can't ever get out of my mind.

Mom asked me if we could stop and get a barbeque sandwich, but it looked really crowded, so I just drove past and told her I could come back tomorrow or another day to get her one, so we stopped at McDonald's drive-through. She liked strawberry shakes and a hamburger item called the Big and Tasty. When someone you love asks you for something or to do something for them, you need to do it for them as soon as possible. You may never have a chance to do it again, as in my case. The same thing happened every night. We had dinner, watched movies, and drank iced water. I would bring Mom to the kitchen table and count out her medicine for her and read the Bible with her occasionally and then go to bed.

We would talk about God every day, though. She talked about God more now than she ever did. I thought at the time that it was just because of the trauma she had been through in the hospitals the last three or four years. Not to mention all the other times before—'80s, '90s, and the beginning of the 2000s. We got up Tuesday morning, she liked Maxwell House instant coffee. Water had to be boiling hot, though. I had it ready for her and had her medicine laid out. I helped her to the breakfast table. I know she had a light breakfast that I prepared, but I can't even remember what it was right now. The store IGA always had freshly cooked chicken, so I bought some of that for our dinner that night along with side orders. I cleaned up and told her I was going outside into the screened sunroom for fresh air. I had a headache. I wasn't sleeping too well. She said she would come outside and sit with me.

We were talking about different things. It seemed like her color was coming back in her face really well. It was getting pretty late that Tuesday night, so we decided not to watch TV. I still got us some iced water and got her medicine ready for her, the nighttime dose. For some reason, she asked me, "Can you read some of the Bible to me?"

Again, I denied my mom and told her I didn't feel too good and that I would read tomorrow. I was the reason Mom wanted to get baptized. I feel now that I did not fulfill my duties as a Christian, a loving son, to deny her something so simple but yet so sacred. The Lord says, "Where one or two come together in my name, I will be there." Yet, I did not know that was the last chance that I would ever have with my mother to ever be able to read to her anymore.

I gave her medicine and helped her to bed. Then I fell across my bed and tried to fall asleep. I didn't even take off my clothes. Wednesday the fifteenth, approximately 7:30 a.m., I heard something moving around in the house. It was Mom. She was in the bathroom with the door shut. I called out for her and asked her if she was okay. The door opened, and she was very wobbly. I helped her to her bed. She sat on the side of the bed. I told her I didn't hear the bell ring that she was supposed to ring for my assistance. She said she didn't think of it.

I asked her if she was okay. She was looking down at the floor while sitting on the bed. I said, "Is it your lungs again?"

She told me, "It's something worse." Right after she spoke those words, her head jerked backward, she fell straight back on the bed, and slid off onto the floor. I screamed for her. I had a handheld cordless phone in my hand. I called 911 for Camden Police, an ambulance, whoever would answer. There was a busy signal on 911. I hung up and dialed again. Still a busy signal.

Mom was not breathing. I remembered the direct police station's phone number. I called them and told them what happened and what was going on. The lady was telling me how to do CPR, and she was sending an ambulance. I heard a loud knock on the front door. There was the chief of police there and other EMT men. I directed them to Mom's bedroom where she lay on the floor. The chief picked up the bed and threw it aside where he could have more room so he could do CPR on my mother. The time had to be around 8:00 a.m. He told the EMT to get a stretcher in there.

They put my mom in the ambulance and rushed her to the Camden Hospital. I got my keys and wallet and locked up and was right behind them with both barrels smoking, meaning I was driving extremely fast. I arrived at the hospital, which was only approximately four to five miles away from Mom's house. I came in, staggering, full of tears, in regret of not knowing how to bring her back or actually knowing what actually happened to her. A couple of the emergency technicians were standing in the hallway outside of the operation room where they were trying to revive Mom. I was really losing it at this point.

They said I could not go in there. I told them I had power of attorney, and they said the doctor had to do his job and couldn't be bothered. I looked at my watch. It was 8:32 a.m. then. The doctor came out of the swinging doors and looked at me one time. He had a funny look on his face and just kept walking down the hall away from me. I screamed out, "What is going on?" I burst through the doors anyway.

There was my mom, lying on a table with a tube stuck down her throat, and a nurse standing there. I said, "What's going on? Why is that tube in her throat?"

She said the doctor pronounced her dead at 8:30 with congestive heart failure, something that everyday medication with nitroglycerin in it could have prevented. The nurse told me that the tube going down her throat was to get air out of her belly. I told her that her belly was always that big because of all the ruptures she had. Mom only weighed one hundred and sixty pounds at that time and was five feet, two inches in height. But she had ten hernia surgeries, and the last one, the tenth one, was ripped out again. You can just imagine why her stomach was so big.

I asked the nurse what was going to happen now. She asked me if I had a funeral director. That's when I broke down again. It's not because I did not want the responsibility of taking care of my mom until the end. It's just that I didn't know that it was going to come so soon. We had a lot of plans we were going to do together. I drove from the hospital directly to Plunk's Funeral Home about two miles away. He was walking in his door the same time I came walking up. I was crying, and he helped me inside.

It took a while for me to pull it together, but I had the money in the bank and wanted to take care of all the business myself right then and there. He started showing me pictures of caskets. The only thing that came to my mind was white like the purity of my mom and purity of Jesus. So I ordered a white nine-gauge steel, white satin inlay, and a Monticello vault. Tim also told me in Camden cemetery he owned a plot he would sell to me for two hundred dollars. That's another thing I wish I had not done in life or did more research on, and that was buying the plot from him. It turned out her plot was actually a walkway in the cemetery. I did not know there were two other people buried on both sides of her. There were no monuments at the time. So when it came time to buy my mom's grave stone, I could not get a standard large size because of the other two burials next to her.

But anyway, when all was said and done, I gladly spent well over eight thousand dollars for Mom's burial, funeral, and the whole nine yards. I came straight home from the funeral parlor and called my one and only dear friend in Chicago that used to play in a band with me, Chris. He knew my mom personally. My mom had cooked for him and laughed and talked with him.

I told him what had happened. He told me he would be there right away from Chicago. He brought his fiancé, Jeanette, the next day. She was Filipino. She was uneasy about staying at my mom's house, so she stayed in a motel we got her just outside of town. She was very superstitious about being or sleeping somewhere that someone just died.

Tim Plunk asked me if I wanted to have Mom cremated. I said no, that I couldn't set fire to anyone's flesh who I loved or anyone, period. Mom died on Wednesday the fifteenth and was buried on the eighteenth in Camden cemetery. That was on a Saturday. I remember Tim Plunk giving me a chrome-plated shovel. I just did as my heart followed and put the first scoop of dirt on my mother. Besides calling Chris, I called my mom's brother, Larry. I don't know why I did it, and thinking now, I should not have done it because Mom told me that when she died, she did not want a lot of people standing and gawking over her, and that's just what Larry made happen. People that didn't even care about her, people that didn't even know her, people that I didn't even know showed up. It was like a dog and pony show, but people that should have shown up, like her two daughters, did not.

I only had the phone number of one of my sisters that used to live with this guy, Doug, I called him. He was very heartbroken. He loved my mom, and my mom thought a lot of him also. He was a very hard worker when he was with my sister. I don't know why my sisters were like this to my mom because she broke her back for them all of their lives—staying up all night ironing their clothes, polishing their shoes, curling their hair the night before with bobby pins, and the next day, taking the bobby pins out and brushing their hair. I witnessed this all of my younger years of my life. My mom also took care of me the same way. Mom would do without to make sure we had something. Talk about being dishonored.

Before the funeral, my mom was brought to the funeral home. After her being embalmed, which I don't know if I should have done that either, they brought her in one room with a closed door. There she lay on a concrete slab with white linen draped across her. This was before the funeral. Chris and I both went down to see her. In this lonely cold room, there she lay.

Chris and I both started crying. Tim asked me if she had a hairdresser. I gave him the name of her hairdresser so Mom's hair would look nice, and a man by the name of Bobby Shannon and his wife, Joanne, said if I didn't mind, they would like to contribute a burial gown for her. It was a beautiful royal blue with sequins, something like the queen of England would wear. Tim also said that we should put some makeup on her for a little bit of color. Mom did not wear much makeup, and I do regret not observing as they put the makeup on her because when I saw her in her casket during the funeral, it was way too much makeup, and I knew she would not have liked it, and it was not the right shades also.

I gave Tim a mother's ring I had bought for my mother with her stone and three children's stones in it, her gold watch I had bought her earlier on, and a gold heart locket necklace. They wanted pictures of her to put on a video screen, so I supplied all pictures of her with me only. Also, I had laid out the first Bible in large print that I had reconditioned and sent to her and knew it meant so much to her, not only because I gave it to her but because it was large print so she could read it clearly. And after studying the words of the Lord in the New Testament, she believed with her whole heart, mind, body, and soul. And those words convinced her that she needed to be baptized.

That was a great day after her baptism. I took her to a fifties restaurant and took pictures of her posing with a mural of the Fonz outside of the building and later brought her back to my townhouse in Bolingbrook, Illinois. I'm so glad I got pictures of the baptism and everything with Mom. Here is what she wrote in her Bible: "Inez French's Bible given to her by her dear and only son, Michael French."

Also, she wrote "Inez French was baptized April 10, 1995—five days after my fifty-ninth birthday in Lockport, Illinois, Church of Christ."

The last day of the funeral, people were asking me, "Is there a will? Whose name is on the will? And did Mom have any money in the bank?" A bunch of money-grub-bing, no-good, evil people were flocking me left and right. My blood started to boil. I just told them all if they didn't sit down and respect my mom at this funeral, I was going to tell them all to get out, and this was the only and last time I was going to say this.

It was time to close the casket and give one last look at my mom. Only a couple of people walked up to her casket, including me. Tim Plunk asked me if he should take her jewelry back off and give it to me. I hesitated in answering him. He said then it would be the only time that I would have to do this if I wanted to do it. Then I started thinking about what the Bible says: "Ashes to ashes, and dust to dust." And I knew from what the New Testament told me that when we die, we are in God's presence until Judgement Day, and that has not come yet. That's when no one will be on the earth anymore.

When Jesus comes back, then we will all have to stand in front of God on Judgment Day to be accountable for everything we've done in life, good and bad. From what I understand in the New Testament, if it weighs more bad, God will say, "Away from me, I never knew you." So Mom is in the presence of God at this time. I did, in fact, have her jewelry taken off for me as a keepsake. Those mate-rial things don't matter to God anyway nor to me. It was just a fact that I gave them to her, and she had worn them proudly. So I had Mom buried on the eighteenth of July 2009 at the Camden Cemetery. Chris had gone back home.

About a week later, I was looking over Tim Plunk's invoice to me and what it had cost me. I was very confused when I ran across one part of the invoice that stated that I had paid one hundred dollars for a limo to carry flowers. I called Tim and asked him about this matter. He said it was the car that carried the flowers. I said, "*What flowers? I'm the only one that bought flowers.*" It was a large wreath laid on top of her casket in the hearse. No one else brought or bought or gave any flowers at my mom's funeral.

I had pictures of the whole funeral in the church and at the gravesite that Chris's fiancé, Jeanette, had taken for me. I guess this is just one way people get away with overbilling if you don't check your receipts and have proof of what happened. He gave the money back to me. If they overbill you through the mail, they could be in a lot of trouble if you know the right people to talk to. They could face up to ten thousand dollars in fines and five years imprisonment for each account. This is considered mail fraud.

By the way, 99.5 percent of everything in this book is videotaped and or tape-recorded or both. Just a warning for people who might see their names in this book and want to challenge me. This might result into, for the person who challenges me, a lengthy court proceeding and, of course, you might guess from yours truly, a countersuit. This is not just because I like to keep my safety deposit boxes and so forth flooding to the seams from recorded backup files or evidence, if you will. *It is because it's hard to trust anybody anymore to keep his word or say the right thing.* So I guess for this reason, I have to help them remember!

I had to call Tim one more time. I told him I would pay him if he would ride to Paris with me because I had to pick up my car and bring the loaner back. I couldn't drive both cars myself, so Tim said he would do it. He said he did not want any money. I offered again, and he said no, so I thanked him.

I had to stop at Fast Trip gas station on 641 Highway in Camden and get gas. I pumped the gas, then leaned in the window and asked Tim if he needed anything from inside. I ended up paying for the gas and buying Tim and myself a soda. I got back into the car and proceeded to Paris. At this time, I had kind of long hair. I was going to cut it earlier before my mom passed away for the Kids for Cancer for wigs. But at that time, my mother said not to cut it because I would not look like Michael then. But with this long hair, I guess it made me look not like a calm person would, but more on the wild side. These are just my thoughts.

Tim Plunk confirmed my thoughts by asking me on the way to Paris if I knew where to get him some smokes. I looked at him and said, "I didn't know you smoked cigarettes."

He started laughing and said, "Not cigarettes, I *mean pot.*"

I asked him why.

He then said, "Sometimes, in my profession, I have to deal with a lot of weird things."

I asked, "What do you mean?"

He proceeded to tell me that one time there was an accident, and he had to put the person's head back on the body and all kinds of other gory things. I did not know where to get pot because my mother and I stayed to ourselves. We had enough to deal with, our mental and physical problems, and I myself even now at this point in my life do not hang around unsavory types of people. But at that time, with Tim, I was so upset thinking about him standing over my mother, smoking that stinking pot while he was embalming her. All kinds of thoughts were going through my mind. I was so mad thinking about a dope head smoking that crap, standing over my mom and giggling. But I kept my cool.

Now I had the walkway that was not a real grave, him trying to rip me off of a hundred dollars for flowers, and the giggling idiot sitting next to me, talking about pot. To me, that's not any respect for the dead. And by the way, the Church of Christ gave him the building he was using for his funerals. I have to be honest, I don't know if any money switched hands, but it's not my concern. One thing that is my concern besides the other three things is that Tim Plunk presented himself to me, the whole town—oh, and I forgot his rotary club that he always bragged about, he represented himself to be a member of the Church of Christ. So anyway, to make a long story short, I told Tim to give me a day or so, and I would ask around for him to see about his pot. *The only reason* I told him that was because I did not have my tape recorder or video apparatus on at that time. I needed time to get wired. I called him the next day, and he was at his cabin somewhere in Benton County on the river or a lake. I can't remember exactly where he said it was.

I wanted to get him in a conversation about the pot that he wanted to buy from me or for me to get some for him from somewhere or some person. So when I called him, I did not know the prices of this stuff or a proper name that was labeled on each type of pot, so I played it the best way I could. And this is what I said to him and what he said to me.

I asked him how much he wanted. He said about a quarter pound, which means four ounces. I asked him how much he was willing to spend. He said he wanted some real good stuff. I told him that I thought it was probably really good stuff. I told him that I was going to work on getting the quarter pound for him for about four hundred dollars.

He said, "Make sure it's good stuff." He was very excited and asked me what time I could get this. I told him I didn't know and that I would have to make some calls. This was on approximately the twenty-seventh of July 2009 at approximately 10:00 a.m. He also noticed that my throat was kind of hoarse. I told him it's been like this for about a week or so. It felt like there was something in the back of my throat that I could not swallow. It just stayed there.

I told him I was going to get it checked out at the VA in Nashville and not to worry. He then said it was probably a lot of stress from my mother passing away. And I was thinking to myself, *Yeah, right!* Not to mention all the other sleazeballs and bums that were trying to come into my life at this point.

I really started thinking about things my mother had told me, and she was right. He then asked me if I needed the money first for the pot.

I said, "No, I'll take care of it myself, and you can reimburse me later."

He then said, "Call me when you get it, and I will give you directions to my cabin" and I should stop and pick up some beer when I'm bringing the pot. He really had this planned out, and so did I because remember, this time I had recording devices going and recorded every word he said. This is the only reason for this call to him, but I did not call him the next day and not answering my phone that day, it rang off the hook all night long.

So the next day when I called him, I told him something very bad happened. I said the guy that had the pot got busted. He was very upset. I recorded this conversation also. I did, in fact, talk to some retired police officers about this incident. They told me not to worry and don't talk to him anymore because he was being watched very closely. That ended with Tim and Plunk's Funeral Home.

10

The Dark Dungeon

I got an appointment with an ENT at the VA on or about the first of August in 2009 because now the only way I can describe the way I was talking or trying to talk, I sounded like the old *Godfather* movies where the Godfather would talk very low in a raspy voice, and me being a singer, it was very terrifying to me. *Pain!* Yes, there was a lot! It felt like I was trying to swallow sandpaper at this point. So at the VA ENT, they sprayed my nose with this liquid that deadened my whole nose and throat. I took my finger and touched my nose and couldn't feel it. It didn't even feel real.

The doctor stuck this long but skinny wire-looking thing in my right nostril and down my throat. This tool that he used had a camera on it, and it was plugged into a monitor. He told me to look at the monitor screen. You can't even imagine what I saw. It was the size of a queen olive, if you know what that is, or radish with bloody mucus all over it. He told me there was also edema present, which is liquid from your body. He brought another female doctor in there. She looked at it and said to me, "We need to get you in for a biopsy as soon as possible."

This is one time in my life that I felt honored by the VA hospital and safe. I reported in a couple days later as told. I can't remember the exact date, but I do know I was pretty scared, and one main reason is the toxic water at Camp Lejeune and some of the things that could happen to a person that were only there for thirty days. *Me!* I was there about two years!

So anyway, I spoke with the doctor during the day of surgery. She told me that if it came back malignant that we would have to start chemotherapy and that it could very well be from the toxic water. The anesthesiologist came in, and I don't remember a thing until they were waking me up. The doctor came in shortly after and told me not to talk, and they took the whole tumor out of my throat instead of just a piece for a biopsy. It would be about a week until they knew the results from the biopsy.

I did not have anybody at all in my life that I could trust except for Chris in Chicago, but he had his own life also, and I didn't want to keep disturbing his routine. He had a lot of responsibility at his job and his home life as well as his baseball card shop that he owned with his brother. I felt that he had helped me more than enough with his friendship, kindness, and money that he had loaned me in the past that I was slowly paying him back as I could. He knew it cost me a lot for my mother's funeral, but that was okay. I did not need that much to live on.

I also paid a driver that I did not really know to come to the operation and to drive me back home, being that they did not want me to drive after that procedure was understandable. I got home finally that night to a very lonely house. I walked around to each room and looked in Mom's bedroom, at her unmade bed, and her porta potty in the bathroom that I had not cleaned out yet. For some reason, I just did not want to. She was my best and only friend that I could really talk to and trust. I know I had Chris, but my mother raised me from a baby. The best mother a son could ever want.

I got some water and went to my bedroom and got back up and went to the living room and laid on the couch next to where Mom sat in her chair along with our iced water we used to have with hard candy. Mom called it the TV candy. The dish was still there on the coffee table with some of her open wrappers. I could not digest everything that had happened to me over and over and over since boot camp. I knew I had to be very cautious out in this world alone, no one to express your feelings with, like Mom, and I thought that if I did express my feelings to anyone, how could I trust them with anything I said? How would I know that they had any compassion for my feelings or be concerned? And I mean really concerned about what I said. I just said to myself God is the only one I can trust because I am not of this world. I can't be. If I could be of this world, I would be doing the despicable things that I have seen done to me and other people.

It says in the New Testament that if you are of this world, *you are not of me! and if you are of me, you are not of this world!* You know, I saw on a biker's vest one time a hand with a middle finger sticking up. I asked the biker what the letters on that patch meant. The letters were FTW. He told me that meant "Fuck the world."

I am not of this world or anything in it. I carried on very nervously every day, thinking about what the results would be of this biopsy. It was about three or four days after my throat operation that I spoke about earlier. I got a call from my ENT doctor at Nashville VA, and she said that I was okay. The polyp that was in my throat was benign. So now I had benign polyps in my colon taken out, benign polyps in my throat taken out, but both the cancerous type, and they warned me to keep a constant check on both for any unusual signs such as blood in my stool, especially dark red, tasting blood in my mouth, any uncomfortable pain, out of any ordinary pain, which in my opinion is no pain.

The doctor told me to go to audiology and dermatology. She noticed the spots on my face. I set an appointment with dermatology. Now I had been there before, and they gave me some type of a topical cream for my face and told me to stay out of the sun, but this time was different. They said the sores, moles, or whatever they were, was crusty, and they wanted to take some type of a tool and burn them off with a laser diode. So they proceeded to do that on my face, neck, forehead, chin, nose, and some spots on my arms and chest. I went to the release of information about a week later and found out that they had written in there what they were burning off was precancer. They called it actinic keratosis, which is one stage below melanoma but just as serious if not more. They were doing the laser procedure, plus they were giving me topical creams such as ketoconazole cream. My body just froze.

And in audiology, they told me that I had vertigo, and that would explain being dizzy at times. They put me on a motion sickness pill (called Meclizine). But the problem with this medication is that I personally think that you should not take this all the time every day. You should only have it when you feel the symptoms occurring. This medication called Meclizine is also prescribed to people that have motion sickness, so therefore, there is a controversy about this medication and how it is prescribed. For example, if you and your wife were going on a cruise and you knew ships gave you motion sickness, you would only take it at the time when you realized it was happening to you. You would not take it continuously a week prior, a month prior, or a year prior of your vacation cruise. Let's see now, what other fine gifts can I expect coming my way as far as my physical and mental well-being is concerned?

11

Digging Deep

I was fortunate enough to find a Nashville directory with yellow pages, and my mission was to find a civilian attorney that knew about the military and VA. Now I lucked out finding Joseph Calendriello. Now I had spoken with Joseph before, and he said he wasn't taking any new cases, but I could call him for advice about filing for disability. Joe told me in 2007 how to file and where to go to file, and that was the federal building in Nashville, Tennessee. That's also where I met Frank Budd in charge at Nashville DAV. But the DAV said I needed more evidence. So at Joe Calendriello's advice, I hired a private investigator.

She came to my mom's house in Tennessee and told me it would be three thousand five hundred dollars to get this information for me. And the information that I was seeking was anyone that could witness what happened to me and everyone that was involved with Sergeant Johnson's court martial. I did, in fact, obtain the men that were in boot camp with me, Forrest and Beaver. At this point in time, Forrest was still a sergeant major in the Marine Corps, and Beaver served four years in the Marine Corps and then twenty in the army. I got notarized signed statements from both of them stating what they saw me go through, especially when I was sodomized by Sergeant Johnson with a baton. They stated they saw me ordered to stand at attention with my bloody boxers on.

Also, I obtained records from Company Commander First Lieutenant D. M. Wells and Series Gunnery Sergeant A. J. Advincula, who were involved very heavily with the court martial and investigation of DI Sergeant Johnson. When asked by my private investigator, when Forrest spoke with my investigator and asked about Johnson, he said, and I quote, *"Oh, you mean the abuser?"*

So when all my documents came back notarized and certified to be the truth for my witnesses, I headed to Nashville to the federal building where the DAV was with both barrels blazing. It was about 87.6 miles from my mother's house. I made it in about an hour. I parked the car, got my parking pass, and proceeded to go in. I met with the people that worked with Frank Budd and brought my evidence to attach and reopen the file that was filed in 2007.

I headed back home to Mom's house. About three days later, I got a call from Frank Budd. He told me I was approved for 100 percent service-connected disability with full benefits. He said that within one month, I should start getting my pay and my backpay from 2007 when I filed. I was told to go to the VA hospital and bring the paperwork that he was sending me to let the hospital know that I was 100 percent service-connected unemployable. I was very happy to finally achieve something that I rightfully fought for. An honorably discharged 100 percent service-connected Vietnam-era Marine Corps vet. I did, in fact, feel honored, but yet did I know about the darkness that was going to come my way again.

Now prior to this accomplishment, if you will, I had a very good psychiatrist, Dr. Small, who diagnosed me for having PTSD (Post-Traumatic Stress Disorder) from the incident with Sergeant Johnson. Only now am I beginning to understand the meaning of PTSD. Also, major depression, nightmares, I guess, and flashbacks of what had happened to me. I was also labeled with agoraphobia, which I found out means I don't like to be around other people or crowds, which is very true.

Bipolar was one of the diagnoses also. They experimented on me with quite a few medications. Ones that seemed to work was Ziprasidone for nightmares, Lorazepam for anxiety, and Lithium Carbonate for mood stabilizing. With 100 percent service disability rating, I could get the rest of my medical treatment finally accomplished, or this is what I thought. I went to the dental and explained to them and showed them my papers that I was rated 100 percent service-connected and I wanted my implant surgery set up as soon as possible. To me, it seemed like they were displeased, and the head doctor came in when I was speaking with the other doctor, threw my file down on the table, and said with an arrogant and smirky smile to me, "So you finally slid through the cracks?"

I said to him, "I don't know what you're talking about, but I'm only here to get what I am entitled to, and that's my implant surgery."

He then tried to scare me. He said that they would have to cut part of my leg bone out, then grind it up to put in my lower jaw bone because my jaw bone was too thin for the implants. Then he also said we could use cadaver bone in a bottle, but I wasn't scared. I told him, "Do whatever it takes to get the job done or I will have to make a complaint with the DAV." They didn't expect that.

Within one month or so, I was set up for implant surgery, but in fact, I thought it was for the ground up bone to be put in my jaw. The day that I went in for what I thought was for cadaver bone surgery or whatever all of the doctors were standing around for and nurses, they told me that I did not need to rebuild my jawbone. It was okay. So like I said before, this was some kind of a cheap low-down scare tactic for them not to do this particular surgery on me. Now keep in mind, this is only words, but each time with these doctors, I learned to carry a tape recorder in my boot or somewhere on my person each time. I was not going to have anyone tell me something and then change their story on down the line. So I got into the chair, the doctors numbed my jawbone and my face, stretched my lips out super wide, and I was awake during the whole surgery proceedings, but I did not feel anything, no pain whatsoever.

They split my gums top and bottom wide open and jerked along my bone line, I guess to clean the bone. I could feel the tugs, but I didn't feel any pain. Then they drilled into my jawbone and placed the implant with some type of socket device and screwed it into my jawbone. After that, they placed what they called a healing bunt on top of the implant, then sewed my gums back up. They explained to me that it would be eight or nine months before I could have the actual implant tops put on. They packed my jaws with cotton and sent me on my way.

Now I feel like this VA hospital has honored me somewhat. The next line of business was to speak to my primary doctor about my joint swelling. Also, my vision was becoming blurred. I was passing blood dark blood, mostly during my stools.

These sores are coming back on my face and arms again, which they called precancer. I have degenerated disc disease. I don't think they can do anything for that. I will have to find out later. My primary doctor from a blood test diagnosed high uric acid in my body, which means that I have to take Allpurinol and Indomethicin for gout. My knees, my wrists, my toes, and my ankles all swell. He also gave me Furosemide to relieve some of the water in my body. This time, I'm five eight and a half and weigh 165, but it's still hard to get around sometimes. He was concerned about my toes and sent me to a podiatrist. Dr. Byron was his name.

As soon as he saw my feet, he said I was a prime candidate for bunion surgery. This entailed the extraction of both big toes, cleaning out the joints, implanting rubber balls, and then sewing on my big toes with sugar thread. He wanted to do this operation right away. It scared me to death thinking about having my toes cut off.

I knew I wanted to move out west, but I did not know where exactly. I needed to be by good VA hospitals that would honor the vets. I obtained an appointment with an optometrist. He said at that time that I needed cataract surgery. That's why my vision was blurred. I asked him how serious it was, he made a joke and said if we were both leaving the hospital at the same time, that he would want a head start before we left, so I would not be on the road with him at the same time. Not having anyone close to me to drive for the operations, I also wanted to postpone this for the new VA hospital I was going to go to. I obtained all of my diagnoses from the doctors and compiled them so I could present them at a later date.

My primary doctor was also concerned about my wrist pain. He sent me to the bone and joint specialist, and then I was diagnosed with carpal tunnel. I guess just like the old saying goes, when it rains, it pours. I needed to get my dental work completed before I could do any of these other operations, secure someone that was dependable and pay them—if, in fact, I was going to get the operations done here—to transport me in my vehicle.

It was getting close to the end of the year 2010 when the dentistry called me at the Nashville VA. They wanted to set me up with an appointment to remove the healing bunts and replace them with the studs that the dentures would snap onto. Upon receiving my studs, they had to make a mold of my mouth and the studs so that they could make the snap-in dentures. I think it was about the middle of October in 2010 when this was completed. I could actually eat again. Not only food like steak but cold food like ice cream without feeling any pain. There were some minor adjustments to be made, but it all turned out well.

(I THOUGHT??) My right ear was hurting so bad at different times it felt like someone was sticking a hypodermic needle into my eardrum. Audiology said it was probably vertigo, but he didn't know for sure. Since I had the back, the bunions, the carpal tunnel, and gout, they prescribed me a cane that I had to go pick up at the ortho department and take lessons on how to use it. They also prescribed me Hydrocodone, which made me sick to my stomach, so a lot of times, I would gag and throw up. Although, earlier in 2010, they also diagnosed me with acid reflux and prescribed me Omeprazole, which I don't think actually did anything for me.

The Indomethicin, which is an inflammatory like Aleve, I don't know if any of my readers ever took an inflammatory. But if you did, you would have experienced a burning sensation in your throat and in your stomach if you did not have food with it. I made the mistake of taking one with a little water in my bed while lying down. A couple minutes later, I felt a strong starchy burning pain in my throat. This happened quite a few times before I realized what inflammatory medicines do to you—your stomach, colon, and so on. I have noticed that I have more frequent bleeding episodes from my rectum during a stool. I noticed it on my toilet paper and in my stool in the toilet. I could see the water turning a reddish color, and the stool was real dark.

Dark blood tells me this is internal bleeding. Nashville tells me it will be four or five months for an endoscopy and colonoscopy to see if I have any polyps again. So I will probably just wait until I get moved and let my new VA hospital take care of these operations and such. I will keep taking and drinking carbonated water to get the gas out of my stomach, but who was I to dictate how the doctors instructed me? For I myself am not a doctor. I just know my own body, though, like everyone should. I will reveal in the latter part of this book of why I just made this statement, so hold on tight, and I mean really tight.

Company Commander First Lieutenant D. M. Wells-
was in charge of DI Sergeant Johnson's court martial.

Series Gunnery Sergeant A. J. Advincula rank in 1973-
was in charge of DI Sergeant Johnson's court martial.

Sergeant Major Richard Forrest rank at present time, was a fellow recruit that endured pain and witnessed my pain and abuse from DI Sergeant Johnson.

Private Joseph Beaver rank in 1973, was a fellow recruit that endured pain and witnessed my pain and abuse from DI Sergeant Johnson.

12

Why Do They Want to Kill Us in Our Own Country that We Defended?

It was the beginning of December 2010. I remember I was having coffee around 10:00 a.m. when I got a call from the social security office. They introduced themselves and then asked to speak with Michael French. I acknowledged my name to them. They then explained why they called. This is what they said. They told me that they could not give out my whereabouts and gave me a number to call, which was the commander's office at the Camp Lejeune Marine Corps Base. So in turn, the commanding office at the Marine Corps base was trying to contact me.

The only reason that I could think of why they wanted to contact me was they said that they overpaid me at Camp Lejeune when I got out in March of 1977. I thought about this for a couple of days and decided to call that number. When the lady answered the phone, the lady identified her department as Camp Lejeune Water Contamination. She gave her rank and name, but I cannot remember it right now. I told her about social security calling me and giving me this number. She asked for my name and my MOS, which means job description when I was in the Marine Corps, and the years I was at Camp Lejeune. She then said, "Hold on for a second." Then when she came back on the phone, she said I was lucky that I called because the Agency for Toxic Substances and Disease Registry, which is referred to as ATSDR, said I was listed to be in the top ten of personnel contaminated at Camp Lejeune because of my records and job description of where I was and worked upon the base.

She then asked me how my health was doing. After explaining to her about the cancerous polyps in my throat and colon and the actinic keratosis on my body, she then told me that I had digested toxic water chemicals. One of the class of chemicals that I was exposed to was known as volatile organic compounds (VOCs) in the drinking water distributed by these two Camp Lejeune water treatment systems. These VOCs were commonly used as solvents for cleaning machinery and weapons, for dry cleaning, and some are found in fuels. She was highly concerned about me and suggested that I register with her department right away! So I did.

I gave her all of the information she asked for: addresses, phone numbers, and so on. She also asked for next of kin or a close friend's name and number in case of death. I asked her why she said death. She told me that these chemicals were very dangerous if digested by anyone. She also told me that she was sending me some information and a letter concerning me, and that I was supposed to take the letter to my VA provider or any doctor I was seeing outside of the VA. She wanted me to keep her updated with anything through treatments or procedures or anything that my doctors found in the future.

I thanked her and told her I would talk to her later. Upon getting off the phone, I was in a daze, like in another world. This really distorted my thinking. I was counting the minutes and waiting for my toxic water mail to arrive. I was pacing the floor all day and all night long. The only thing I could think about was the beginning of DI Sergeant Johnson and the hell he put me through then. And now, I had cancer cells living in my body. So what's in store for me in the future to come (if there is any future)?

About a week had passed, and I finally got the information from Lejeune. I read through this and found out a nightmare that was existing, another thing that the Marine Corps had accomplished for me and other people, civilians and marines and navy personnel, whoever: watch out having children; there could be birth defects. Men, start measuring for bra sizes, for now you could be growing breasts. There are neurological behavioral effects. The list goes on.

Now it was up to me to work close with my doctor to find out what gift I was going to receive next. I found out that Nashville VA did not know too much about the toxic water, but my doctor was trying to do research on these matters for me and other patients. I asked him if there was any way or anything that I could take to dilute these chemicals from my body. He told me then that the Arizona VAs were more abreast to resolutions for these matters and that I would have to move there in order to be treated. I also was told that President Obama was very concerned about the troops and their families that this toxic water contamination had affected. After all, this great president was the reason that the men who were affected by Agent Orange were treated and determined what percentage of their body was to be documented as disabled.

I had confidence in President Obama. He also was responsible for anyone returning from war or service-connected psychological and physical conditions. Psychological and mental, meaning PTSD. President Barack Obama was really helping our nations troops. He really cared. He was really on top of things all the time. He demanded answers for why these chemicals were in the water system in the first place. When and how did they start?

I knew I had to do something and do it fast if I wanted to live longer. My primary doctor at Nashville VA had been sending me every week to get blood tests at the lab. My uric acid was up, so that meant more pain with the gout. He said that my blood count or cell count had changed on each test, and he wanted to find out why. But I wanted to go to Arizona to where they said in Nashville that Arizona VA was really up on this toxic water stuff. I made my phone calls periodically.

I also contacted real estate agents from different real estate companies to find out how much houses would cost close to the VA hospitals and what the taxes would be out there for a 100 percent service-connected disabled Vietnam marine veteran in Arizona. I pinpointed Phoenix and Tucson, also surrounding areas to these two cities because Phoenix and Tucson were the two cities with VAs that had knowledge of this toxic water poisoning at Camp Lejeune, North Carolina.

I spent most of my time seeing my doctors at the Nashville VA, also in touch with the toxic water contamination department at Camp Lejeune, and the lady there suggested that I contact the Bell Legal Group in Georgetown, South Carolina. She told me that this law firm was taking on cases concerning anybody that suffered physical or mental problems from these toxins that were put in the drinking water at Camp Lejeune for thirty years. I said to *my astonishment*, *"Thirty years?"* I then said, "What do you mean?"

She told me that the chemicals or toxins that were discovered in 1987 were put in the water systems from 1957 to 1987. And I was there for two years from 1975, 1976, and March of 1977. She then told me that if anyone was there more than thirty days in between 1957 and 1987, they would more likely be contaminated. I almost passed out hearing these words.

Did the Marine Corps think that the troops or somebody at Camp Lejeune knew something that was top secret? Or were they sending people they didn't like there to be killed? The Marine Corps has a motto: Death before Dishonor. As I think about this motto, what does this really mean? Does it mean that we will kill people before they dishonor us? I sure hope in God's name this is not what's going on in our country that we defend.

13

Nowhere to Run, Nowhere to Hide

W ell, it was January 2011, about a year and a half after my mom passed away. So many things had happened. But one thing that had not happened was answers being given. Yes, answers! And what I mean is *somebody* has to know or have somewhat of a clue about who was responsible for letting all those chemicals go into the drinking water for *thirty years!* What about the EPA? What about the commander of the base that did not get poisoned by these chemicals? Were only the important people's water purified? All the high-ranking officers' water purified? And maybe the congressional guests at Camp Lejeune, was theirs purified?

I do know for a fact that people just turned their heads when I asked these questions. And I do also know for a fact that myself and all of my friends that were enlisted rank, WE are important! So where was our clean water to drink, bathe, and cook with?

I had already called Bell Legal Group, and they sent me a form to sign, which I did. Below is a form that Bell Legal Group had filed for me. They assured me that this would not or never will be a class action lawsuit. By the way, tape recorders and video equipment are a great investment because sometimes people forget promises they told you or very important things that could affect your life. So I would like to think the reason why I use these items is because I'm helping people retain good character by refreshing their memory and keeping them honest. At least today's world should be done this way, in my opinion. You can't trust a person with their word or a handshake anymore.

So back to what people assure me when I speak to them. Below is a claim for damage, injury, or death, and this is Claims Department OJAG—Navy:

CLAIM FOR DAMAGE, INJURY, OR DEATH	INSTRUCTIONS: Please read carefully the instructions on the reverse side and supply information requested on both sides of this form. Use additional sheet(s) if necessary. See reverse side for additional instructions.	FORM APPROVED OMB NO. 1105-0008

1. Submit To Appropriate Federal Agency: Office of the Judge Advocate General (CODE 15) Claims and Tort Litigation 1322 Patterson Avenue, SE, Suite 3000 Washington Navy Yard, DC 20374	2. Name, Address of claimant and claimant's personal representative, if any. (See instructions on reverse.) (Number, Street, City, State and Zip Code) Michael French c/o J. Ryan Heiskell Bell Legal Group, LLC Georgetown, SC 29440

3. TYPE OF EMPLOYMENT X MILITARY ☐ CIVILIAN	4. DATE OF BIRTH	5. MARITAL STATUS	6. DATE AND DAY OF ACCIDENT 1955-2000	7. TIME (A.M. OR P.M.)

8. Basis of Claim (State in detail the known facts and circumstances attending the damage, injury, or death, identifying persons and property involved, the place of occurrence and the cause thereof. Use additional pages if necessary.)

Claimant was at Camp LeJeune in 1975, 1976 and 1977, where he worked as a truck driver. He previously had cancerous polyps (1987) in his throat and colon. He also has severe vertigo, which makes it hard to eat anything and keep it down, and he feels at times like he has an ice pick stuck in his ear, causing severe pain. Claimant believes that his health issues are more likely than not related to his exposure to contaminants found aboard Camp Lejeune.

------AMENDED CLAIM------AMENDED CLAIM------AMENDED CLAIM------AMENDED CLAIM------

9. PROPERTY DAMAGE

NAME AND ADDRESS OF OWNER, IF OTHER THAN CLAIMANT (Number, Street, City, State, and Zip Code).
N/A

BRIEFLY DESCRIBE THE PROPERTY, NATURE AND EXTENT OF DAMAGE AND THE LOCATION WHERE PROPERTY MAY BE INSPECTED. (See instructions on reverse side.)
N/A

10. PERSONAL INJURY/WRONGFUL DEATH

STATE NATURE AND EXTENT OF EACH INJURY OR CAUSE OF DEATH, WHICH FORMS THE BASIS OF THE CLAIM. IF OTHER THAN CLAIMANT, STATE NAME OF INJURED PERSON OR DECEDENT.
Claimant previously had cancerous polyps (1987) in his throat and colon. He also has severe vertigo, which makes it hard to eat anything and keep it down, and he feels at times like he has an ice pick stuck in his ear, causing severe pain. Claimant believes that his health issues are more likely than not related to his exposure to contaminants found aboard Camp Lejeune.

11. WITNESSES

NAME	ADDRESS (Number, Street, City, State, and Zip Code)

12. (See instructions on reverse.) AMOUNT OF CLAIM (in dollars)

12a. PROPERTY DAMAGE	12b. PERSONAL INJURY	12c. WRONGFUL DEATH	12d. TOTAL (Failure to specify may cause forfeiture of your rights.)
	$30,000,000.00		$30,000,000.00

I CERTIFY THAT THE AMOUNT OF CLAIM COVERS ONLY DAMAGES AND INJURIES CAUSED BY THE INCIDENT ABOVE AND AGREE TO ACCEPT SAID AMOUNT IN FULL SATISFACTION AND FINAL SETTLEMENT OF THIS CLAIM

13a. SIGNATURE OF CLAIMANT (See instructions on reverse side.)	13b. Phone number of person signing form	14. DATE OF SIGNATURE 2/3/11

CIVIL PENALTY FOR PRESENTING FRAUDULENT CLAIM	CRIMINAL PENALTY FOR PRESENTING FRAUDULENT CLAIM OR MAKING FALSE STATEMENTS
The claimant is liable to the United States Government for the civil penalty of not less than $5,000 and not more than $10,000, plus 3 times the amount of damages sustained by the Government. (See 31 U.S.C. 3729.)	Fine, imprisonment, or both. (See 18 U.S.C. 287, 1001.)

95-109   NSN 7540-00-634-4046   STANDARD FORM 95
PRESCRIBED BY DEPT. OF JUSTICE
28 CFR 14.2

This book—my book, my title—*Honorably Dishonored* seems to be the start of my life when I entered the Marine Corps. I hope at this time, you are absorbing in detail what you are reading because it's just a start of you understanding what I meant by *Honorably Dishonored*. It started with boot camp with penicillin shots, to DI Sergeant Johnson, being threatened before his court martial, all the situations that happened to me in the Marine Corps. This toxic water mess happened to me while I was in the Marine Corps, but I did not know it at the time. *But* when you turn to read the very last page of my book, you will definitely know the meaning of *Honorably Dishonored*.

So now I had to get to Arizona where the doctors knew more about this, the toxins in this water. My thought was to try to dilute these chemicals from my body somehow, some way. That would be my discussion with the VA doctors in Arizona.

President Obama was supposed to be sending some literature from the US Department of Veterans Affairs concerning Camp Lejeune Water Contamination Historical. From what I understand, he thinks like me and ten thousand more marines because he said how could this be going on this long without anyone knowing about it? Thirty years? Something's wrong with this picture, and I mean really wrong.

I have been talking with a couple of my high school friends, and they told me about one guy, Eddie, and gave me his number. Eddie also was in the Marine Corps about the same time I was and at Camp Lejeune. Eddie will die soon if he does not receive a new liver transplant from a donor. That's what Lejeune did to Eddie.

I did find a website with videos of CNN, MSNBC, and other Marines and civilians that were talking about being exposed to this toxic water poisoning and the effects that it has on their health, the illnesses they have from the toxins in the water. Others were in tears talking about their dead children because of this. Anyway, it is so disgusting. But here is the website, www.tftptf.com. The "tftptf" of this website means The Few, the Proud, the Forgotten. This is a perfect website for what's going on here at Camp Lejeune.

Now once you get on this website, here is what you should do to watch videos. (1) Look at list on the left and scroll down; (2) click the word *Videos,* and that takes you to a page with a list of videos. You can click on any video because all of them discuss Camp Lejeune and the victims and survivors so far to date of what these people have done to us. If I didn't have a personal relationship with Father God, my Lord and Savior, Jesus Christ, and the Holy Spirit, I know for a fact I would not have this driving force that keeps me motivated. Well, I've got to get checked up with every one of my doctors here in Nashville and obtain some more information about the VAs in Arizona. What I do understand is that the Phoenix and Tucson VAs are abreast of all of these poisons which are tetrachloro-ethylene, trichloroethylene, benzene, vinyl chloride, and dry-cleaning fluids; and from what I also understand, they know how to deal with humans that have digested these toxins, absorbed through their skin, and so on.

So right now, I'm concentrating on real estate agents and homes in an area that's not congested. Well, tomorrow I have to get back to the Nashville VA. They are going to burn some more of these actinic keratosis sores, which is called precancer, off of my body with a laser diode. It's kind of painful but well worth it if it is going to prevent these from turning into melanoma.

You know it is pretty surprising to me and anyone that might know something about me, which is only a handful after that boot camp thing. I prefer to stay quiet and just to sit back, watch, and listen. But actually now, and I don't understand it with all of these things wrong with me, I'm full of energy. I still hurt a lot all over my body, but I still have a high amount of energy. I'm sure that God really has a plan for me. And he is why that I have, only through him, an explosive and dynamic energy force. Unlike my poor friend, Eddie, with the liver problem, hepatic steatosis, that was also caused by toxic water poisoning at Camp Lejeune. This poor guy is my age, but the only thing he talks about is dying. At least before I get off the phone with him on each call, I always have him laughing a little bit before the call is ended.

I love to make people laugh because at the age of seventeen, there were too many tears, confusion, and pain. I get about three and a half to four hours of sleep every night, waking up drenched with sweat, and then paced the floors, trying to understand the dreams I had. Some of them I do understand. In some of them, I'm dreaming about doing everything all over again in boot camp.

I've had one dream twice, and I never want to have this dream again. I dreamt that I signed up with the Marine Corps for six more years. I don't know how I got there. I did not know the people around me, but I was in the commander's office. I don't know where. I only knew it was on a Marine Corps base, and he was explaining to me that I was in for six more years. The only thing I remember about those dreams, except for while still sleeping in my bed, was fighting to get awake, fighting to get out of the dream, slinging back my covers, drenched in sweat, trying to get my bearings together.

In this dream, which was the second time with this dream, it seemed like a long one. But when I looked at the clock in my bedroom, I remembered going to bed around 11:00 p.m. The time on the clock said 1:25 a.m. when I woke.

The doctor has given me Prazosin for nightmares and Lorazepam for anxiety, but I usually dream almost every time I go to sleep. All except for the nights that my body is really drained from staying awake a night or two with no sleep. This medication is not really working. This is the only time when I am totally exhausted that I can get some what rested. No matter what I try, I cannot get Johnson out of my mind. If I see a state trooper, I think about him because troopers wear the DI hats. Any uniformed man, war movies, Jeeps, trucks, the color olive drab, combat boots, and when I hear someone say yes sir. I have some things from the Marine Corps that I keep private, only for my eyes, and a brother Marine that has gone through the same things that I have. I really don't like to speak of my past in the Marine Corps, especially when it comes to the cruel sexual abuse and beatings from DI Sergeant Johnson.

As far as parents, young men, and women: parents, investigate all avenues of anything that your children want to be involved with. Whether it is Marine Corps or summer camp, get to know and be a close part of your children's lives. As far as the young men and women, the same principles applies to you. In this world today that we live in, if you practice what I'm telling you, it might save you a lot of grief and disappointment and maybe even your life. It is not wrong to be cautious and ask a lot of questions. If someone gets sick of you asking questions, you don't need this situation in the first place.

My mom used to tell me, "Mike, *don't put your business in the street!*"

I asked her, "What do you mean?"

She said, "People do not need to know everything about you." And she further explained, "Your savings account, where you keep your class ring when you're not wearing it, when we are going on vacation." Basically, she was preparing me for this crazy life that we live in these days with identity theft, home invasions, and the list goes on.

Although there is one thing that she explained to me that she said would make her very happy. She had a big smile on her face as she began to tell me, so I asked her, "What are these things that would make you happy?"

She told me that she would like for me to be a witness and testify. I knew what those two words were and what they meant from watching TV. She told me to be a witness for something great, something honest, something pure, something that I agreed with when I witnessed. She also said that I should testify. Testify means to tell the truth and the whole truth without leaving anything out about anything or any topic, which means do not add any words or take away any words.

She had me scared at this point. So I asked her, "Am I supposed to be going to court for something that I don't know about? Is that why you are telling me this?"

So then Mom started talking about God and his love, and when she said that to me, she did not have to say anymore. Because when you know and believe in God, the Son, and the Holy Spirit the way that we do, it will be automatic for you to be a witness for God, Jesus, and all the things he has done and what he is going to do in the future when he comes back for us. We now have faith, so we witness for him and testify everything he says he is going to do, that what he says is the truth. We may be helping someone that doesn't have as much knowledge about him as I do or someone that doesn't know anything at all. We could be helping them. Or someone that doesn't believe.

So we stand up for Father God, our Lord Jesus Christ, our Savior, and the Holy Spirit. So with this in mind and all of the positive points I have learned in life, I decided to go to Arizona and look at some homes.

14

One Step at a Time

After obtaining the plane tickets for Phoenix, Arizona, I started loading my car with suitcases and my carry-on laptop. In August 2011, here in Tennessee, it gets very hot and humid. I had to change my shirt two times because it was 110 degrees humid and about 100 degrees hot, so I kind of chuckled when I thought about what people said about Arizona's weather.

The real estate agents told me it was very dry heat with low humidity around Phoenix. They told me I could live healthier out there. I proceeded to Nashville's airport. After boarding the plane, it was only about two hours, and we started to descend at Sky Harbor Airport in Phoenix. The skies were pretty and blue, and the city was spread out. I picked up my luggage on the carousel and proceeded to the rental car place. Then off to Highway 17 North to Bell Road.

I rented a hotel room on Bell Road for one week. That is where my real estate agent told me to go. I called him to let him know I was there. He was supposed to have about a dozen houses for me to look at. He called me back at my room and said it would take him a couple of days to get all of the information ready for the homes. So I waited a couple of days, and then on the third day, I called him back. He explained to me how sorry he was and said he would be in my room the first thing the next morning at 9:00 a.m. I was pretty upset at this time because I only had three days left to stay before I had to catch a plane and go back to Nashville. He did show up the next day and said he had got a couple of places that I would really like.

I got in the car with him, and we drove about forty miles west of Phoenix to a town called Tonopah. No stores, one gas station, and a lot of dust. Yes, the house looked okay. It was a Santa Fe style built in 2005 with 1,500 square feet, a two-car garage for $85,000, but it was not for me. So he brought me to another house in Tonopah, and this house was definitely not for me. To make a long story short, since he said those were the only homes he had to show me, I told him that he was not for me. So I decided to look around myself.

I met a few people and got ready to head back to Tennessee. So this right now confirmed another thing my mother had told me, and that is don't believe anything you hear and only half of what you see. I'm still determined to find a house out here because of this toxic water poisoning and the toll it is taking on me. From what I was told about the VA from different sources, but never actually been to the Phoenix hospital, it was all to the positive. So after landing in Nashville, I retrieved my car and started heading back to my mom's house, which was my house now, but I like to think of it as Mom's.

I went into the house and made some coffee and listened to the answering machine, and to my surprise, the same realtor that I went to see had a message for me. He said he had found more houses for me to look at. Did he think that I had wings or somehow could transport myself back out there without spending any money? I just laughed to myself. He had already honorably dishonored me, just like the rest. I started thinking the only one you can depend on is Father God, Lord Jesus Christ, and the Holy Spirit. With that in mind, I tucked myself into bed.

The next day, I awoke and decided to look for homes for myself on my laptop. I taught myself how to pull up the map of Phoenix on my laptop but towns not so far away and desolate, like the real estate agent brought me to in the town of Tonopah. I needed access to the VA hospitals, grocery stores, things of the nature. Here in Tennessee at my mom's house, the VA is approximately 87.6 miles away. There are quite a few fast-food places, two grocery stores, and a Walmart Supercenter within three miles away from the house. This is what I had to keep in mind this time and obtain more information for my search. Also, I knew I had to sell my mother's house, so I found a real estate agent after talking with about a half dozen of them. Jon was his name. He seemed like a very nice guy, a Christian and a family man.

We started to make plans on how to show the house, some strategies when the time came to put it on the market. There wasn't too much to be done in that house. I replaced the carpet, put tile in the other rooms, a new roof, new blacktop driveway and paint inside. It was red brick on the outside and a solid little house. I also replaced the field lines for the septic tank. So the house was ready to go.

I made a promise to my mother to not let any of our possessions be sold or given away, which I would not do anyway. So I will have a lot of things to move when the time comes and a lot of planning to do. I also promised my mother that we would have a gravesite together. This meant, that after I got settled, I would have to exhume her body, buy new plots, and have her placed in her final resting area. But a promise is a promise.

Well, the holidays were beginning to roll around. Thanksgiving would be in about two weeks. I was thankful, in my opinion. I had the best mother a son could ever want. I had Mom's recipes for a great Thanksgiving dinner, but I didn't feel like cooking. It would be a waste to cook a whole turkey just for me. I guess I needed to find something to do during these holiday times.

Being alone here by myself just made me depressed without Mom around. At least I had good memories. After four hundred and twenty-six songs I had written in the past, they were all copywritten through the Library of Congress in Washington DC, and I am affiliated with BMI, National Songwriter's Association, but since Mom's passing and a short time before that when she was sick, I have not been able to write a single song. For some reason, about a week before mom did pass, she told me to never stop my music. Now it is different without her.

Although I pick up the guitar now and then, no songs really come out. I guess I really haven't been trying hard enough. But I can't say that either because I really didn't have to. The songs just flowed like a stream. I used music to escape from the reality of what happened to me in boot camp. I used anything to escape from the reality of what happened to me in boot camp. Not just boot camp, the whole act of duty in one big ball of crap. Oh, well, Thanksgiving passed now. All was well, but everything was still dragging along, so I started experiencing with my laptop. It's amazing how many things you can find on here.

I was speaking with Chris the other day on the phone. He told me I should try one of these dating sites. So I tried one of them and filled out some things about myself. They wanted a profile, but I wasn't going to give all of my personal information. The first day, I got what they call invites. This thing was pretty wacky, but it was something silly to do. So I left it alone for a while. I would check it each week and see who wrote me a letter or something or a note.

*****

Well, it was Christmas tomorrow. I would celebrate Jesus's birthday or the day that we honor for his birthday. I think I will start tonight and watch some of the old Christmas movies that I bought for Mom and some of the old pictures I will look at from when I was really young. Mom used to love taking pictures all of the time. A lot of people would say that they would like to go back and start over with what they know now, but not me. I definitely would not want to endure any of the bad things that I have been through or take a chance on it. I really feel in my heart that everything happens for a reason, and I also feel that it's our job to seek out what that reason is. I don't like to ask for too much when I pray. I just thank Father God for Jesus and the Holy Spirit. That's why I am writing this book, to explain and expose some of these wicked people that have been in my life and others that were with me.

I'm sure a lot of people can relate to this book. But it's not over yet. I have just let you find out a few things that were terrible, horrible, and wicked. Some of the worst things are yet to come. Just keep reading if you've got the stomach for it. But I do cherish the pictures my mother took.

15

New Year, New Beginnings

Well, it is January now, and snow is still on the ground here in Tennessee. Now I found out that I now have gout arthritis for sure, and the doctor has prescribed me Allupurinol and Indomethicin, which is inflammatory. It is not working so well and burning my stomach.

I told him, and he said, "Just keep taking it and eat food with it."

But really, it is still not helping the burning sensation. I'm also taking Omeprazole for acid reflux, not to mention about twenty other medications. They have a pill to go to bed, a pill to get up, a pill to eat, and a pill not to eat. A lot of these pills will make it blurry to see. I think I was a lot better not taking any pills. I've got a pill to crap and a pill not to crap. I wish they would make a pill for the doctors to take which would make them think better because all these pills I don't think are healthy for my body.

I've got a pill for my flashbacks, my dreams, but they don't work. I've got a pill for depression, and when I think about all of these pills, I get more depressed. These pills do not stop the reality of what I went through. Talking with my doctor, Dr. Small, helps me, but now he is leaving the Nashville VA. Speaking with my mom helped me a great deal, and also speaking with God helps the most.

*****

Well, the seasons are changing now. Now we are looking at March. The grass is starting to grow. I don't know if I can push the lawn mower this year. I am going to call some landscapers and see how much it will cost. I contacted a company called Two Men and a Goat, and for fifty dollars, they would take care of my yard, per mowing. I should say Mom's yard. Because this gout in my toes, ankles, wrists, and knees, not to mention I have carpal tunnel and two bunions on my big toes, a doctor wanted to cut my toes off. Dr. Byron Nashville VA in podiatry showed me the rubber balls that he wanted to insert into my joints and told me we could do it right away. He said he would sew my toes back on with sugar thread and give me Velcro-like shoes, but I was scared. He wanted to do both of them at the same time.

I have nobody to drive for me. That would be 87.6 miles to my house. I told him I wanted to wait until I moved to Arizona. The toes are inflamed from the bunions and gout. So Dr. Byron gave me a foot fix kit to present to my new doctors, explaining his diagnoses.

I'm so glad I found the landscapers because sometimes I have to hold onto the walls when I get out of bed going to the bathroom because my toes are so inflamed and swollen and red from the gout and the bunions, not to mention the rest of my joints. I don't know if this is all due to toxic water poisoning from Camp Lejeune. I don't have any direct answers. That is why I am seeking help in Arizona where they claim to have specialists for these situations concerning toxic water poisoning, TCE, PCE, vinyl chloride, and benzene. I mentioned earlier about the online dating sites.

After conversing with several women—that I will not call ladies; most of them were gross—a lot of them wanted money from me. They gave me sob stories about how their car was broken down. They said that their ex-husbands weren't paying child support and that they needed money for their kids, etc. But much to my surprise, the last of March 2012, I conversed with a lady on the dating site. On this site, you can put a picture on there of yourself, but this person only put a pair of eyes. I thought that was very comical, yet she spoke with me, and finally, on my private e-mail, we spoke more in-depth and exchanged phone numbers. We had a lot in common. Music is one of the main things, and she was very concerned about her salvation and wanted to learn more about Christ, our Lord and Savior.

We spoke on the phone for the first time on April eighth, and she told me that she wanted to be baptized after reading the chapters I told her about in the Bible. She came to see me from Illinois, and that was another thing that we had in common. She grew up only about one hundred and twenty miles away from me where I lived in Illinois. This was the end of May when she came to see me with her friend. I let her and her friend sleep in the spare bedroom. She only stayed overnight and had to go back the next day.

We stayed in close contact over the phone, and since we had so much in common, we decided to join forces to speak all through the summer. Stephanie came to stay with me in June and helped me with things. She is a great caregiver. So we got together at Mom's house and searched for homes all through Arizona and Nevada. And then in August 2012, I got notice from Toxic Water in Camp Lejeune that President Obama signed a letter, saying "On August 6, 2012, President Obama signed into law the Honoring America's Veterans and Caring for Camp Lejeune Families Act of 2012. For Veterans who served at Camp Lejeune between 1957 and 1987, this law provides VA health care for fifteen medical conditions. Support for health care costs may also be provided for family members for these conditions once Congress appropriates funds and new regulations are published."

This notification will be included in a direct copy in this book. This will be scanned in. My condition was worsening, so Stephanie and I decided to go look at the houses in person in Arizona and Nevada. We took flights to both states. With no luck, we came back to Tennessee. We kept looking on the Internet to find a home that would fit our needs. I called a real estate agent to see if he would go in person to videotape the home that I found in Casa Grande, Arizona, which was in between Phoenix and Tucson, both supposed to have high-grade hospitals. He videotaped the house and sent it to me. We set a date to go look at it.

Stephanie and I flew in person to look at the home. It seemed to be perfect for what we wanted. They wanted 179,000 dollars, and I offered 160,000 dollars, and they accepted. So February 28, 2013, we went to the title company, filled out the necessary documents, and got the keys for our new home.

Now still owning Mom's house, it was up for sale. I had a lot of upgrades in Mom's house but I did get the money that she initially paid for the house. For being 2013, the market was so low that I could not get more. One thing that really disturbed me is that State Farm Insurance insured Mom's home. We've had State Farm since I was ten years old, but these agents tried to rip me off. When I bought the home in Arizona, they canceled my insurance in Tennessee. I asked them why because I still owned the home. They thought that since I bought the new home that I did not need insurance in Tennessee. So when I told them to reinstate the insurance in Tennessee, they tried to charge me more. I had a big fight with these people. That's another honorably dishonored situation. I will have another book on these situations coming out after this book, number one concerning State Farm Insurance and other dishonest companies and people that dishonored me.

So I am going to end this chapter with a sigh of relief only because I'm going through all of this again. All these situations actually haunt me, but the worst is yet to come. *And I'm not done yet! I would not let them forsake me nor anybody else. I'm finished with people doing these situations to me. I will include all of everything that I am saying is a fact. You decide if I am right or wrong. Videotapes and tape recordings don't lie.* My girl, Stephanie, tried to erase the bad things in my life and the bad things that might be coming, but she's only a girl. She has not manifested herself yet into becoming a woman in the world. She is still soft. I cannot blame that on her. It's still too easy to get over in life. It hurts her sometimes when people talk to her abruptly when she is only trying to do right. I am sorry for her. Let this be the end of this chapter.

16

Heading West

After five thousand miles back and forth with moving trucks, Stephanie and I are finally settling into our new home. I failed to mention earlier that I took Stephanie on February 10, 2013, to be baptized into the Church of Christ. This is where you are added and you do not join. Only God can add you. So this means that our relationship is *strictly platonic.* If I want God to bless us, this is the way it has got to be until marriage. We are both very much okay with this.

For the first week here in Casa Grande, Arizona, it is where I checked into the clinic. I told them that the main hospital I needed to have was in Phoenix. I went to the Phoenix VA hospital. I could not believe my ears of what I was hearing or what I was seeing from other vets and personal experiences from the doctors. All the scuttlebutt, which means gossip, was going around everywhere about how they were not helping the veterans and killing them. They would not give me any of my prescriptions from what I had at the Nashville Tennessee VA, and how I know this is because they called me on my phone. I explained to the secretary of Dr. Hightower—a female doctor at the Phoenix VA who is going to be working on my scripts, about twenty-two to be exact—that I was a 100 percent service-connected unemployable disabled veteran from the Vietnam War.

She laughed at me over the phone and said, "What does that have to do with anything?"

I told her then that I was going to report her. About a half an hour after that phone call conversation, I received a call from the Phoenix VA Campus police, security, Boy Scouts—whatever you want to call them. When I answered the phone, he asked me why I was harassing the girl in question. I told him I was not harassing and that I have everything on tape recorder, that I just wanted to be treated and done fairly. This conversation with him was also tape recorded.

Then later on that night, I saw on the news where Judge Jeanine Pirro had done investigations. So quickly, I said to myself, "I have got to go to a different VA." So I transferred to the Tucson VA—*honorably dishonored again!* I reported to the Tucson VA to get checked in. I explained to them about my toxic water poisoning. They had no inclination of what I was speaking of. I brought them a letter that President Obama had sent me, and it did state, in fact, that anyone that was stationed at Camp Lejeune for thirty days or more was subject to this fatal disease. I was stationed there about two years—bathing, washing, drinking water, or digesting, if you will, these chemicals that are benzene, vinyl chloride, TCE, PCE, and dry-cleaning fluid chemicals, which has caused me to have cysts in my right kidney—twenty-two to be exact—according to the doctor, hepatic steatosis, blood cells inadequate, renal toxicity.

Upon all of this information, I was transferred to a new doctor, which was Dr. Neustat. This drug on for about two months. I in turn had gone and filed a complaint with Senator John McCain's office in 2013. *Nothing was done at that time, and each time I called, they said they were working on it.* Upon seeing Dr. Neustat, he called me aside in the hallway from the waiting room to his offices, and in a low verbal voice—which I have recorded and is very audible on my recordings and, in fact, he scared me to death—he told me *if I didn't get this stuff checked out that I was playing with fire.*

Let me ask you a question. How am I supposed to have anything checked out unless it was doctor's orders? They exclaimed that I had blood in my bladder, polyps in my colon, and abnormal white blood cells that were mutating. I pleaded with them to please take care of me and find out how I can be healthy again. From that point, the Patient Advocate Office explained to me that Dr. Neustat did not want to be my doctor anymore. There is more on my tape recordings than what I am typing right now in detail that I will explain later on in this book. Recordings, videotapes, progress reports, and documented doctor's notes and lies—like Susan MacDonald and Julianne French—will be accessible in CD form and DVD form.

Besides that, I called back Senator McCain's office where my complaint was filed in 2013. They said they were working on all of this. Maybe they were thinking that this toxic water poisoning would be fading out all of the soldiers and conditions that pertained in this era, just like Agent Orange. Well, as of now, it has not faded me out. This has only driven me to the course of finding out why I gave my life for this country, and they decided to wash away this problem, and thanks to President Obama, he is trying to help.

I love President Trump and what he stands for. I hope he does get wind of this book. I would like to see what his take would be on this. I guess maybe they think that anybody that was in this era would be dying out. *But don't forget that there are real people out there, relatives or friends, that cannot let this go of what is happening to me. I declare my statements here now to be procured in the history books of America, truthful and honest. In the name of the Father, Son, and Holy Ghost.*

I was able to get an appointment through Dr. Neustat to see if I had a blood clot in my right leg. But I had been bleeding from my rectum bright red and dark red blood in my stools. I repeatedly asked for an endoscopy and a colonoscopy.

Not only with the blood coming out of my rectum, I feel a brutal pain in my intestines below my belly button. They knew I had cancerous polyps taken out of me in 1989 by Dr. Sauder in Jackson, Tennessee, nine to be exact, and in 2000 at Hines VA. In February of 2015, Dr. Neustat set me up for a consult with gastroenterology. On February 13, 2015, I had an appointment with Dr. Beaumont in gastroenterology. He told me they would be calling me back in a couple of weeks and not to stop my painkillers because they would take care of everything. They would have to put me under during endoscopy and colonoscopy.

Well, everything is looking up as far as the treatments and procedures for my gastroenterology problems. I called in the middle of March to speak to Dr. Neustat and have been wondering why was there a hold up on them calling me for my procedure in gastroenterology. *Finally*, on May 28, 2015, I got a call from Elaine in Special Procedures Unit about my colonoscopy and endoscopy. *My up and coming appointment in August? What the hell is going on?* I'm thinking.

She said because there had been some changes, she wanted me to call her back at 520-792-1450 at extension 4890. So I called her right back. She said there would be no doctors in July and August, that all of the gastro doctors had left. My thought was, *Did it have anything to do with a vet a couple of blocks from me who had died during a procedure because they took out too much of his intestine?* I don't know. But this sure looked scary to me.

So she set me an appointment for June 12 at 10:30 to report to a GI. I don't know how much blood is in me and how much I can bleed or if there is real cancerous polyps in me now. All I know is I'm in pain and getting the run around from this VA once again. And to this day, they called and left messages on my phone, which I still have, saying that they have no doctors to perform this. This was from 2015 to 2018.

Sometime around May 15, 2015, I stubbed my two toes next to the little toe. Dr. Neustat sent me for X-rays and an MRI on my right foot and ankle because I had unbearable pain and could hardly walk. My two toes looked broken and were slanted toward the big toe and still are to this day. On May 22, 2015, I got a phone call from M. Martinez-Garayzar about the results. In my progress notes of what he told me they said, PT contacted and instructed on right foot MRI results with metatarsal fracture. PT advised that podiatry consultation was placed for further evaluation and treatment of fractures. PT stated pain to right Achilles. PT instructed to discuss foot pain with podiatry at time of evaluation. PT verbalized understanding.

Dr. Neustat then set me up a consult to see Dr. Felix Jabczenski in podiatry and orthopedics clinic, which I saw on July 7, 2015. Why so much time in between notifying me about my accident and the x-rays, and then Dr. Jabczenski? I have no idea. Not to mention the gout arthritis and bunions that I was dealing with in both feet, my ankles, and all of my joints all over the body with gout arthritis. I have carpal tunnel in my wrists. The only thing they did for this was give me a cane, wrist braces, ankle braces, and pain pills. This was not doing anything for me. The braces were only hindering me from being mobile and quite dangerous. The cane, and sometimes pain pills, help me, but they don't take it all the way. I need operations.

Later in this book, you will find out more about Dr. Jabczenski, if that is what you want to call him. At this time in my life, I was not flagged. Up until today, the present time, I still have to walk with a cane or hold on to the walls and the furniture going to the bathroom in the morning, and you will find out why later on in this book the reason. In between all of this unorganized, untimely mannered wish wash that I'm getting from the VA, I got a call from nuclear medicine for my heart also on May 22, 2015. Dr. Walsh in Nuclear Medicine is who I spoke with. I wanted to know if the nuclear medicine that they wanted to put in me for the stress test would hurt me in any way because of my toxic water poisoning.

First, he said it would not hurt me. Then he started explaining what it was and that it had radiation in it. He said then he would have to find out. He wanted to do some checking on it. I never heard back from him. Neustat then set me up with Dr. Keldahl, a urologist. My appointment with him was on June 10, 2015. He had his face buried into his computer and asked me all kinds of weird questions that I didn't know how to answer. It just so happened I had my letters from President Obama, and I put them on the corner of his desk and said that this is what the president said about all of us that had been affected by this toxic water.

He slammed his hand on top of the papers and crunched the papers in a fist and threw them off in the floor and screamed in a loud voice, "*I don't care!*" He also started yelling at me, asking me, "Do you know how much an MRI costs?"

I was beside myself. So was my caregiver, Stephanie. I was speechless. My Nashville VA was a great VA. Anything they took care of with no questions asked. So was the Hines VA in Chicago. But this was becoming a nightmare. I had nowhere to turn. I just had to take it from them.

Dr. Neustat sent me to the administrative medicines. They were supposed to take care of things like toxic water,

Agent Orange, things of that nature. On June 11, 2015, when I met with miss Mary Gilles, she had my paperwork where Dr. Neustat had verified the diagnoses hepatic steatosis, cysts in my kidneys, renal toxicity, blood in my bladder, and the list goes on. I asked her, "Are you in charge of treatment for these things? Or can you dilute in any way the toxins and poisons in my body?"

She just kind of laughed at me and said, "You can call anytime." And she would start working on everything for me. She said she was very well-informed of my Camp Lejeune toxicity. She said she got most of her information from Dr. Neustat and the tests he ran. She also pulled out a document that was almost identical to the one President Obama had sent me and the Camp Lejeune water contamination people from the registry act of which I am registered. They exclaimed to me that I was one of the top ten that ingested this poison and was contaminated.

I waited about a week and didn't hear anything, so I decided to call her office again. When I did call back, her secretary answered the phone. Now remember, I'm tape recording everything with the one-party consent law, meaning in the state of Arizona federal and state, you do not have to tell anybody you are recording them if you are one in the party that gives consent. Her secretary asked me who I was and my last four numbers of my social security. The secretary got back on the phone and informed me that Mary Gilles said never to call there again.

This really freaked me out. I explained to her that I just saw Mary about a week ago, and she said to call any time. She said, "Mary said do not call there anymore." So

I proceeded and called the chief of staff's office. I reported the incident and explained to them that it was all tape recorded. I spoke with Julianne French in the director's office and reported the incident. I left tons of requests for Jonathan Gardner, who was the director, to call me. He never did call me back. But that's not the only time I asked for Jonathan Gardner to call me. It seemed like it was set in his mind that he was too good to talk to a veteran or any veterans because I spoke with a lot of veterans at the hospital, and they said it was a waste of time for me to try to talk to Jonathan Gardner. Or just maybe, he did not want to get his tit in a sling by being on a tape recorder.

17

Praying for Someone to Care

Now we are going to talk about July 7, 2015, when I first saw Jabczenski. I was checked in and led down a hallway to a separate small waiting room. I was sitting there for over an hour. It was way past lunchtime when I was finally called in, and that was 13:35, or for civilians, 1:35 p.m. I was told not to eat anything in the morning because there might be labs. I was weak from no nutrition, and in quite a bit of pain, but still I felt like throwing up.

Finally, he called me in. He asked me, "What seems to be your problem? Why are you carrying a cane?"

I said, "Take a look at my ankle. You can see what the problem is. It is the size of a large grapefruit. You can't even see my ankle bone. I'm in a lot of pain."

He grabbed my foot and ankle with his forefinger and thumb and started squeezing around different areas. I screamed, "You're hurting me!" My whole foot was inflamed and red.

He said, "I needed to move it more."

I told him, "I tried to move it. It just keeps getting bigger then."

He told me then that I should soak it. I told him I did both hot and cold, but nothing helped. I said, "Isn't there anything you can do for me?"

Jabczenski said, "We can try cortisone." He brought a needle in with cortisone and poked it in my ankle. It was a pain that I never felt before. It hurt so bad I screamed. He said, "That's good. At least we are getting the right area." I was sweating so much then from the pain I felt like passing out. Now here were his notes. I got them straight from the release of information.

By the way, this whole incident was definitely tape recorded and videotaped. Dr. Felix Jabczenski says:

> Subjective: The patient is referred to me for evaluation and treatment of his ankle. He is a fairly healthy 59-year-old, does have a history of gout, but had turned it awkwardly when he was in a grocery store about 4 months ago. Ever since that time, it has been painful and swollen. He had an old injury where he cut his Achilles tendon, but that is healed.
>
> Physical Examination: He walks with a slight limp, favoring his right foot. He is tender mainly over the lateral aspect of the ankle. He has good flexion and extension of the ankle joint. Good inversion and eversion of the hind foot.

Imaging: X-rays were reviewed. They demonstrate some mild subtalar arthritis, but otherwise are normal. MRI shows some swelling in the ankle joint, the old Achilles tendon rupture that is healed, and a questionable fourth metatarsal shaft fracture.

Diagnosis: Mild subtalar osteoarthritis of right ankle.

Recommendation: I discussed treatment options with him. With his consent, I injected the subtalar joint with a combination of Depo-Medrol and lidocaine. I recommend ice, anti-inflammatory drugs, and a follow-up if his symptoms do not improve in 2 months. Felix F Jabczenski, MD.

Well, with the inflammatory drugs ripping the lining out of my stomach and throat, I did, in fact, call him back. They had me come in again for more cortisone or whatever the hell he was giving me. He then told me to keep moving my joints, and it would get better as the time goes on. *Well, it did not.* With repeated calls, I did not get any answers. My frustration was growing, and disappointments were well over hand. I felt pain in my chest. I told Dr. Neustat. He said that I needed an EKG and a stress test with contrast. I said okay.

Now diagnosed with carpal tunnel, bunions on my two big toes, which needed to be taken off and rubber balls put in and my toes sewn back on with sugar thread, gout arthritis, degenerative disc of the spine, I looked like a robot trying to get around. I can't even begin to tell you the amount of pain I felt at this point. Now my chest was pinching and there was a pain going straight from my chest down to my stomach. I don't know how to explain it. It brings me to my knees when this happens.

So I called up and tried to get this scheduled for me. I know it was serious but all this pain at one time could not be good. It seemed like my body was falling apart. I couldn't get a grip on things. I try to ignore it, but it keeps hounding me, and for this reason, my stress rises even more. Who do I turn to? Well, I have been turning to God. I feel calmness with him. But still, the pain is here.

18

Where Do They Get These People? Wasted Time Again

On August 10, 2015, I had a neurology appointment with Dr. Katherine Bonsell. She wasn't even a real doctor. She was a resident training to be a doctor, still in college, and practicing at the Tucson VA. I know she kept going to the front to ask Dr. Bergen, the doctor in charge, for the right answers. And by the way, Dr. Bergen was supposed to be the doctor I was seeing that day. I do not know why I ended up with an inexperienced pregnant woman with emotional problems that hated veterans. She was still in school. I needed a real doctor.

Every time I asked her a question because she was not smart enough to answer herself. She was the type of woman that had her nose up in the air all of the time. She acted like she was the most beautiful person on earth. *Not!* In my opinion, she was as dumb as a box of rocks. What bothered me was how anybody with any intelligence at all could act this dumb. For instance, I was discharged from the United States Marine Corps honorably in March of 1977. She had in my file I was discharged in the 1980s. The next thing she said was that I lived in Tucson.

I lived in Casa Grande and had been ever since 2013 when I bought my home with Stephanie. Last but not least, this person was so mad at me that she was stuttering because of the fact I showed her light bills and my driver's license of where I did live. I did not have anything on my person at the time to show her when I got out of the Marine Corps, but who lies about that anyway?

She got up from her chair and went outside in the hallway and started growling and clenching her fists. And last but not least, she came back in the room fists clenched, veins popping out of her neck, and had to get one more dig in at me. Now I was not smoking then, but she said in a very rebellious way that I reeked of nicotine. I went to the release of information and got all of these facts, but just like usual, nobody cared about doing a thing. After every time I saw a doctor or anybody, I went straight with Stephanie to the Release of Information. On this incident, it wasn't a big deal, but it was a big deal to me.

On August 19, 2015, I tried to report this to Donna Wilson, the Privacy Officer for Tucson VA. Now discussing Bonsell's notes to her and also discussing my toxic water poisoning at Camp Lejeune, nothing was done yet that day, so once again, I had to wait for something to be done.

19

Yet Did I Know I Was Being Set Up

Sometime in September 2015, I called back Dr. Neustat. His secretary or registered nurse Susan MacDonald intercepted the phone call on three different occasions and would not let me talk to Dr. Neustat when, in fact, he told me to call him to get these appointments set up. I explained to Susan MacDonald, and she said she would take care of everything, but she could not answer any medical questions. So I insisted on speaking with him.

My prescriptions were not coming in properly through the mail. So that was another reason I needed to speak with him. He has to sign off on all of them. On September 9, 2015, Susan MacDonald called me back at my home, and my caregiver, Stephanie, answered the phone. But Susan was not prepared to be tape recorded.

I grew up in a day with '65 Mustang 289s, and just before I went into the Marine Corps, I bought a '72 340 Plymouth Duster. All of my friends in school, including myself, all had hot rods, and these cars came from the factory with dual exhausts. You're probably wondering as you are reading this, what does this have to do with the cost of tea in China? Well, it had a whole lot to do with it, especially when you want to defend yourself from any little liar that tries to put words in your mouth.

So I told Susan that day that if I didn't get my prescriptions right and Dr. Neustat didn't call me back that I would jump in my car and be down there in record time with both barrels blazing. Well, there's the dual exhaust again.

About two weeks earlier, I had reported Susan to the chief of staff's office for her not letting me speak to Dr. Neustat. Then I finally got to speak with him.

20

Their Scam Failed Again

On the date of October 14, 2015, I got another neurology appointment set up, and this time, it was with Dr. Bergen, the head neurologist at the hospital. When I arrived there at Bergen's office, she was very nice and upbeat. I told her all of my problems with the pain stabbing in my right ear, the vertigo, and also what student Bonsell had lied about with the year I got out of the Marine Corps, where I lived at, and so on. She said she couldn't quote anything on that because she didn't read the notes of what Bonsell said.

I said not to worry, I had all the notes here. She did not want to see them. She kept asking me questions, one right after another. I could not even give an answer. She wanted to give me a psychological test. I asked her why. She then said it was to get to know me a little bit better. I told her I did not believe that.

The chief examiner in Nashville, who was in charge of determining disabilities, gave me that test. And it says on my disability determination papers that I am permanent and total 100 percent disabled *and I am not supposed to be tested or asked to be tested again for the rest of my life.*

With so many words, this doctor told me that she could not do anything for me. Another wasted visit. You have to watch out who you are dealing with in this life. I don't care what it is from ordering hamburgers to doctors who are trying to scam you for whatever reason to benefit them. In the back of my mind and in my heart, I know what these reasons are and were at the time. I'll explain this in Volume 2 of *Honorably Dishonored*. Well, that is the future. Let's get back to the present.

21

Dealing with the Demons

I then saw Donna Wilson again on another appointment on October 21, 2015, and told her about the Arizona state and federal recording laws and discussed more about getting Bonsell's notes where I lived at, when I got out of the Marine Corps, and me reeking of nicotine removed from my records. She explained to me that in order to correct where I lived at, at that point and the year and time I got out of the Marine Corps, it would be an act of Congress. Then I got a letter from her in November 2015 stating:

> After a thorough review of your written request for an amendment and a clinical review of your records, your request has been granted in part. The physician has agreed to correct your city of residence. However, the reviewing supervisor finds that the information authored by Dr. Katherine Bonsell to be accurate, complete, and relevant in its current form.

Nothing else was taken out of my records. How *stupid* can people be. Don't you think I know when I got out of the Marine Corps? It is on my DD214. But she did not want to see it. I didn't know at this time, but soon I was going to find out that student Bonsell, Dr. Bergen, Primary Dr. Neustat, Susan MacDonald Neustat's assistant, Mary Gilles in Administrative Medicine, Urologist Dr. Keldahl, Dr. Felix Jabczenski in Orthopedics, the gastroenterologist, heart doctors, Patient Advocate Vicky McManaman, Julianne French, Assistant Director, and Jonathan Gardner, the Director, all had morning meetings about different topics on how to save money at the hospital, different patients, who should be treated, and who should not be treated. They were calling the shots. They did not like me calling all the time and complaining about getting something done that was not done. That is why at this time, over two and a half years, nothing at all was done for me except pills and more pills. They wanted to get me off their backs. And very soon, I would find out how they intended to do that.

You see, a person like me that tries to do right—or I should say examines myself very closely to do the right thing—likes calling around and looking in my disabled veteran handbook, which tells me that me as a 100 percent service-connected disabled veteran should in no way be denied any medical treatment at all. It is like having a lifetime warranty on fixing parts on my body. But when you are working with an institution that tells their employees that they will get extra time for a vacation if they can save some money from treating the vets, people like this do not have feelings, moral values, and their hearts do not go out at all for the patients. They just think about themselves. And they are afraid if they rock the boat by treating a vet properly that they will lose their jobs.

22

Exposing the Wicked

In December of 2015, I got a letter in the mail from Julianne French, who I believe was the director's assistant, flunky, or whatever you propose to call her at the Tucson VA. But I do not call her a human being. The letter stated that I was flagged as a threat nationwide to any VA in the country. And when I called other VAs nationwide to see if I could be treated, they exclaimed to me that letter was truthful. I called her up on the phone at the chief of staff's office at the Tucson VA and asked her what this letter was about. Who was I supposed to be a threat to?

She explained to me that I threatened Susan MacDonald over the phone on September 9, 2015, Dr. Neustat's nurse, secretary to my primary doctor, and said I was going to bring guns to the Tucson VA and kill everybody. I freaked out and told her I didn't say anything of the sort or the nature. I don't even own guns. She then said she believes Susan MacDonald, and that is why I got flagged. So now in the back of my mind, I knew this is how they were going to scam me with this scheme of lies in order for them to have a reason not to treat me.

So I in turn went to get my release of information and doctor's reports from my files in my office in my home. I learned a long time ago to obtain my files right after my doctor's visits or any type of discussion on the phone with these people. And what I mean by "I learned" is because if you do not obtain your records right when they are written down, they will bury the records and add something else in just to suit them. This happened quite a few times. I didn't say anything about it. It just taught me that I needed to get my records as soon as possible from A to Z and everything in between because these people will put out *fake news* like our great President Donald J. Trump talks about with the fake news.

This type of thing happens all over all the time. It is up to you to prove your truth because they don't know the meaning of truth. I fear for the day for them when they come in front of God on Judgment Day. So I read my notes and discovered that it was little Susan MacDonald who falsified a government document on September 9, 2015, but on her document that she signed, falsifying a government document, she stated "PT was very upset about refilling his Vicodin and stated he was coming down on Friday with 'guns blazing.'"

Now I realized that a few months prior to her statement date on September 9, 2015, is how they were trying to figure out how to stop me from asking for their services. So at this point, I knew how this conspiracy was going to take place. Every one of these people had conspired against me unlawfully. So I relistened to my tape recording with Stephanie, Susan MacDonald, and myself. Like I said, when I was growing up, my early teenage years, you get used to saying things a certain way, especially when it comes to driving your hot rod cars.

On my tape recording, which is digital and cannot be changed or edited any way, form, or fashion, I said I was going to come down there top speed with both of my barrels (tailpipes) blazing. Nothing at all about guns or killing people was ever mentioned. *I did not make any threats to anybody about any guns blazing at all. I know she was mad at me for reporting her for not talking to Dr. Neustat, but that is not a way to treat any human being and tell lies about it. She is the worst, and this VA is the worst for lying, not treating and cheating vets out of their services, especially a 100 percent service-connected disabled honorably discharged Vietnam veteran like myself.* So I knew at this time I could not go to that VA or any other VA because when I called them, they said I would be arrested on the spot.

Remember, everything that I'm presenting to you in this book is, in fact, videotaped and or audio taped or both. I've heard from time to time again from other vets how situations like this have affected their lives. When I asked them, "What are you doing about that?" they just bowed their heads and shook them back and forth in defeat. And there is more of a lot of them that go through this all of the time.

This has really saddened me to see people with power actually thinking and believing that it is okay to walk through this world, acting in this manner. Myself, I could not do these things. That is why I am exposing them. Just like in the Bible, it tells you in the New Testament:

Everyone who does evil hates the light, and will not come into the light for fear that his deeds will be exposed. But whoever lives by the truth comes into the light, so that it may be seen plainly that what he has done has been done through God. (John 3:20 NIV)

And also in the New Testament, Ephesians explains how to expose evil:

Have nothing to do with the fruitless deeds of darkness, but rather *expose them*. For it is shameful even to mention what the disobedient do in secret. But everything exposed by the light becomes visible, for it is light that makes everything visible. This is why it is said: "Wake up, O sleeper, rise from the dead, and Christ will shine on you." (Ephesians 5:11 NIV)

So that is what I am doing: exposing the wicked. Just maybe, they will turn around their ways and understand what I am trying to convey to them.

On December 20, 2015, I asked Stephanie to call Tucson VA Emergency Room. My chest was hurting really bad. I could not get my breath. My face was really red, and my left arm was hurting. I knew I shouldn't be going to the VA, but this was an emergency in my opinion. I was at the kitchen table, listening to Stephanie speak with the

Emergency Room. I also warned her that she should record the conversation. A woman in the Emergency Room got on the phone by the name of Rita Watson. She told my fiancé, Stephanie, when I thought I was having a heart attack. The words she said to Stephanie and on the tape recorder were, "Is Michael going to come here to the hospital with guns and kill everybody? Because that's what Michael said he was going to do."

Stephanie then replied to her, "What are you talking about? We don't have any weapons."

She repeated, "Well, he said he was going to come kill everybody."

This person was also in the morning meetings with the chief of staff and part of this conspiracy. I never did go to the Emergency Room. Stephanie just gave me some aspirin, and I laid down and tried to forget about all of this mess.

From that point, the next day, I decided that it was not safe at all to set foot in the Tucson VA. No telling what they would do or lie about next. All I knew for a fact was they thought that they had gotten rid of me.

23

Another Politician, Another False Doctrine When Will They Learn They Cannot Keep Lying?

What good does it do them? Does it make them feel big and strong? Do they think a lot of their peers look up to them? I think that they have fallen so far in that they will never ever climb out of the sewer where they live. When I look in their eyes, sometimes our eyes lock together, and it is just like looking into a big room of hate with no feelings, not even for their own selves. You can speak to them, but they do not hear. You can try to compliment them, and they turn away. It is just like the *Night of the Living Dead*, and don't even try to talk about God to them or even say "God bless you" to them. That is when I got the looks that made me feel like they wished I was dead or wanted to kill me themselves.

You know, it says in the Bible, in the New Testament when Jesus came to test the spirits. AND IT SAYS,

> Dear friends, do not believe every spirit, but test the spirits to see whether they are from God, because many false prophets have gone out into the world. This is how you can recognize the Spirit of God: Every spirit that acknowledges that Jesus Christ has come in the flesh is from God, but every spirit that does not acknowledge Jesus is not from God. This is the spirit of the Antichrist, which you have heard is coming and even now is already in the world. You, dear children, are from God and have overcome them, because the one who is in you is greater than the one who is in the world. They are from the world and therefore speak from the viewpoint of the world, and the world listens to them. We are from God, and whoever knows God listens to us; but whoever is not from God does not listen to us. This is how we recognize the spirit of truth and the spirit of falsehood. (1 John 4:1–6 NIV)

On the top of this page, I state another politician and another false doctrine, and my question has been answered when I state right now, when will they stop lying? But at the time of this incident, I did not realize that the truth and an understanding was in a book right above my head each night when I fell asleep. I had to prove my innocence, so I went to a politician, Congresswoman Ann Kirkpatrick. Her office was in Casa Grande, Arizona. Everyone raved about how she could and would help the unfortunate. She had a man there. His name is Palmer Miller. I did in fact videotape all of our meetings and let him know and listen to some of the tape recordings of the hospital staff. He seemed, at the time, laid back and said he would help. Stephanie was with me.

I had two ink pens that could videotape up to three and a half hours. My watch could also videotape in different angles for up to three and half hours, and the most revolutionary digital recorders can record a conversation from now until infinity. When you have equipment like this, and I bought mine at Brickhouse Security, you have true evidence. You cannot alter digital recorders at all. You cannot take out parts, add in parts, change the recording, period.

So Mr. Palmer Miller went in the other room and brought out complaint forms for me to fill out. He said he was going to push this through, that he believed my innocence because, in fact, I played some recordings to him from where Susan MacDonald lied about the conversation on September 9, 2015. He seemed like he was pretty eager to get to the sum of my problems.

I filled out the paperwork and then told him goodbye, and we would stay in contact to see what happens with it. My intentions with it were to prove my innocence, prove that I did not say anything about bringing any gun to the VA, prove that she, in fact, lied against me on a government document, and also her supporters—Miss Julianne French, Administrative Assistant to the chief of staff, Jonathan Gardner, Director of Tucson VA Healthcare System, and Miss Donna Wilson—were involved from me contacting her on August 19, 2015, about a doctor. I'm sorry, Resident Katherine Bonsell did stupid little things just to upset me that were not corrected and should not have been put in my medical record book. I'm enclosing a copy of Bonsell's notes for your records.

These people are so stupid, more than any stupid person that I have witnessed in my life. So I am including in my book my DD214. The time I did and the time that I was discharged from the Marine Corps. Let these nuts put that in their pipe and smoke it.

THIS IS AN IMPORTANT RECORD
SAFEGUARD IT.

1. LAST NAME - FIRST NAME - MIDDLE NAME	2. SEX	3. SOCIAL SECURITY NUMBER	4. DATE OF BIRTH			
FRENCH, Michael	M	████	YEAR ██	MONTH ██	DAY ██	

5. DEPARTMENT, COMPONENT AND BRANCH OR CLASS	6a. GRADE, RATE OR RANK	6b. PAY GRADE	7. DATE OF RANK		
USMC-11	Private	E-1	YEAR 77	MONTH 01	DAY 10

8a. SELECTIVE SERVICE NUMBER	b. SELECTIVE SERVICE LOCAL BOARD NUMBER, CITY, STATE AND ZIP CODE	c. HOME OF RECORD AT TIME OF ENTRY INTO ACTIVE SERVICE (Street, RFD, City, State and ZIP Code)
UNKNOWN	UNKNOWN	421 Kenyon Roseville, Il 60441

9a. TYPE OF SEPARATION
DISCHARGE

b. STATION OR INSTALLATION AT WHICH EFFECTED
RUC 12651
TrkCo, H&SBn, 2dDSG, 2dMarDiv(Rein) FMF CLNC

c. AUTHORITY AND REASON
JFG8

d. EFFECTIVE DATE	YEAR 77	MONTH 03	DAY 18

e. CHARACTER OF SERVICE
UNDER HONORABLE CONDITIONS

f. TYPE OF CERTIFICATE ISSUED
DD-257-MC

10. REENLISTMENT CODE
RE3c

11. LAST DUTY ASSIGNMENT AND MAJOR COMMAND
RUC 12651
TrkCo, H&SBn, 2dDSG, 2dMarDiv(Rein) FMF CLNC 28542

12. COMMAND TO WHICH TRANSFERRED
N/A

13. TERMINAL DATE OF RESERVE/MSS OBLIGATION	14. PLACE OF ENTRY INTO CURRENT ACTIVE SERVICE (City, State and ZIP Code)	15. DATE ENTERED ACTIVE DUTY THIS PERIOD		
YEAR MONTH DAY NONE	Chicago, Il 60607	YEAR 73	MONTH 06	DAY 08

16a. PRIMARY SPECIALTY NUMBER AND TITLE	b. RELATED CIVILIAN OCCUPATION AND D.O.T. NUMBER	18. RECORD OF SERVICE	YEARS	MONTHS	DAYS
3531: Heavy Vehicle Operator	Truck Driver Heavy 905.883	(a) NET ACTIVE SERVICE THIS PERIOD	03	08	10
		(b) PRIOR ACTIVE SERVICE	00	00	00
17a. SECONDARY SPECIALTY NUMBER AND TITLE	b. RELATED CIVILIAN OCCUPATION AND D.O.T. NUMBER	(c) TOTAL ACTIVE SERVICE (a + b)	03	08	10
		(d) PRIOR INACTIVE SERVICE	00	02	01
NONE	NONE	(e) TOTAL SERVICE FOR PAY (c + d)	03	10	11
		(f) FOREIGN AND/OR SEA SERVICE THIS PERIOD	00	11	25

19. INDOCHINA OR KOREA SERVICE SINCE AUGUST 5, 1964
☐ YES ☒ NO

20. HIGHEST EDUCATION LEVEL SUCCESSFULLY COMPLETED (In Years)
SECONDARY/HIGH SCHOOL 12 YRS (1-12 grades) COLLEGE 0 YRS

21. TIME LOST (Preceding Two Years)	22. DAYS ACCRUED LEAVE PAID	23. SERVICEMEN'S GROUP LIFE INSURANCE COVERAGE	24. DISABILITY SEVERANCE PAY	25. PERSONNEL SECURITY INVESTIGATION	
(03) 761001-761004 (02) 761018-761020 (75) 761223-770108 NONE		☐ $15,000 ☐ $5,000 ☒ $20,000 ☐ NONE	☒ NO ☐ YES AMOUNT N/A	a. TYPE ENTNAC	b. DATE COMPLETED 730719

26. DECORATIONS, MEDALS, BADGES, COMMENDATIONS, CITATIONS AND CAMPAIGN RIBBONS AWARDED OR AUTHORIZED

National Defense Service Medal
Sharpshooter Rifle Qualification Badge

27. REMARKS

Enlisted in the U. S. Marine Corps
Issued a military motor vehicle operators permit up
to and including 2½ ton tactical vehicles.

28. MAILING ADDRESS AFTER SEPARATION (Street, RFD, City, County, State, ZIP)

29. SIGNATURE OF PERSON BEING SEPARATED
████

30. SIGNATURE, GRADE AND TITLE OF AUTHORIZING OFFICER
R. S. CROCKER, 1stLt, USMCR, ByDir

31. SIGNATURE OF OFFICER AUTHORIZED TO SIGN
R. S. Crocker

DD FORM 1 NOV 72 214 MC PREVIOUS EDITIONS OF THIS FORM ARE OBSOLETE. THIS IS AN IMPORTANT RECORD SAFEGUARD IT. S/N 0102-002-0001

REPORT OF SEPARATION FROM ACTIVE DUTY (1900) SRB/OQR OR HQMC 2

Progress Notes

Neurology Clinic: Referral/Consultation for new patient

Referring Provider: NEUSTAT,STEPHEN J
Reason for Request: "memory loss, Camp Lejeune veteran"

History of present illness:
Mr. French is 59 year old man who presents to neurology clinic for evaluation of
memory complaints. He also complains of visual problems which he states he was
told were a neurologic problem. Patient is accompanied to clinic by a
caregiver, whom he states assists him with household chores that he cannot do
due to mobility issues. Patient states his memory issues are mainly with short
term memory. He states that he frequently walks into a room and forgets why he
is there and needs to write things down or he will forget them. He states that
the most distressing memory issues are with music. Patient works as a musician
and has forgotten the words to songs when he gets up to perform. Patient is
able to perform all his ADLs, cooks for himself, maintains all the bills for his
home and a second home which he rents, does his own grocery shopping, and drives
without any issues.

In regards to patient's visual difficulties, he reports that beginning in the
1980s he began having episodes of blurry vision and red-color desaturation. The
episodes would last for a couple hours at a time and then self resolve. These
episodes have significantly increased in the past 10 years, and he reports that
they now happen every day, sometimes multiple times a day. As the episodes have
worsened, they are now also associated with headaches. He states that the
visual symptoms precede the headaches, the headaches are right sided "gnawing"
in quality. They also involve a sharp right ear pain with tinnitus. Patient
states that he was prescribed Meclizine for the tinnitus with thoughts that he
had vertigo, however, he denies any vertiginous symptoms. With these visual
changes, headaches, and tinnitus, patient also has associated nausea and
vomiting. The episodes usually last for 2-3 hours and improve with rest. He
states he has increased frequency and duration of episodes when he is tired or
stressed. Patient is on multiple medications for chronic pain including
Indomethacin, Aleve, and Vicodin. He takes the Indomethacin and Vicodin daily,
and the Aleve several times per week.

Patient also complains of right sided facial numbness that has been present
since the 1980s without change, and bilateral carpal tunnel syndrome.

Patient was stationed at Camp Lejeune for 2 years in the early 1980s and was
exposed to contaminated water. He is concerned that these symptoms are all
secondary to that exposure.

Bonsell Notes

Progress Notes

Social History:
Patient lives in Tucson with a full time caregiver
Denies any Tobacco use, but patient reeks of Tobacco on his clothes and on his breath.
Denies alcohol and drug use

Family History:

ALLERGIES:
PENICILLIN

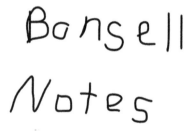

VISTA Electronic Medical Documentation
Printed at SOUTHERN ARIZONA VA HCS

Page 65

I have had nothing but trouble with this VA in Tucson, Arizona. *Nothing but trouble.* Either I don't get the care I need or they are lying about the craziest things like when I got out of the Marine Corps. Don't you think I know when I got out of the Marine Corps? I just wonder about this flock of little girls—Donna Wilson, Kathrine Bonsell, Julianne French, Jennifer S. Gutowski, the acting director, and we can't forget the pride of the pack and number one liar. I think she needs to have a Grammy presented to her, and that would be Miss All Over Herself, Miss All About Herself, *Susaaaaaaaaan Macdonald!*

You see, it started with Susan MacDonald not letting me speak to my primary care doctor, Dr. Stephen Neustat, who explained to me that we needed to start action on the blood in my bladder, the mutating cells, and to call him ASAP and converse with him in the next three and four days or I was playing with fire. This is what came out of my doctor's mouth. That locked me into a very serious mode, a very scared mode. When Susan kept intercepting my calls and laughing at me and would not let me speak to my doctor, I had no choice but to call the chief of staff's office and report this thing. I can't see a person like that being human. But what I did not know at the time when I reported her was that Julianne French, Donna Wilson, Jennifer S. Gutowski, and Rita Watson in Emergency Department were all on her side. Now the little lying girls that we have here are, in fact, the ones that made my life hell when the only thing I was trying to do was be treated for toxic water poisoning in the beginning.

Now let's get this straight and name these whatever you want to call them in alphabetical order: Kathrine Bonsell, Julianne French, Jennifer S. Gutowski, Susan MacDonald, Rita Watson, and Donna Wilson.

So back to Ann Kirkpatrick and Palmer Miller, the ones that tried to help me. Mr. Miller called me down to Kirkpatrick's office headquarters here in Casa Grande and told Stephanie and I to sit down and presented me with a letter from Jennifer S. Gutowski, and at this time, she was the acting director, and it started out to be addressed to Honorable Ann Kirkpatrick.

So Palmer Miller gave me the letter and told me to put it in with my files because I would probably need this in the near future or so. At this time, I had no idea who this Polish woman was. Nor did I know anything about what she might have looked like. But evidently, she knew me like a book. I'm going to include the whole letter with dates and everything but we are going to enter this part right now from the brilliant-minded Jennifer S. Gutowskiiiiii!!! And it says:

> The Patient Record Flag (PRF) on Mr. French's record was entered in response to threatening statements made by Mr. French to SAVAHCS staff. Hospitals are one of the most high-risk areas for violence and the VA has taken steps nationwide to reduce the chance of violence by developing behavioral flags to warn staff of a potentially violent patient who may

pose a risk to other patients and staff Mr. French's case was presented to the Disruptive Behavior Committee which recommended that Mr. French's electronic medical record be flagged after he stated to a staff member he would come down to the VA with "guns blazing." The VA is obligated to provide a safe environment for patients and staff. The VA will continue to monitor Mr. French's behavior and review his case again in two years. If Mr. French has no further behavioral issues, it is likely the behavioral flag will be removed at that time.

Now I need to remind my audience and some of the bimbos, if you are reading, I have three hundred and seventy-eight audio and video tapes concerning any and every matter of my book, and my only wish would be that just one of you would challenge me or try to bring me to court. Because after *my* evidence, I will present you with a countersuit that is going to be heard *around* this world. I have sat back and taken all of your ridiculing, lying, making up false stories, all I'm going to take. In fact, anybody that I have talked about in my book, I'm ready to rock and roll if you are.

Now let's remember one delicate matter. This make-believe world of Susan MacDonald that said and claimed on a government document where she lied and said I was going to bring guns and kill everybody *is a bogus lie.* It's unbelievable this was entered into my records by Susan on September 9, 2015; but the matter of fact is I didn't get a letter until the middle of December 2015. It makes a real man—and I mean a real man, not a lying cheat—to sit back and wonder why in the world that little lying Susan MacDonald or the rest of the lying pack wait to send me a letter four months later, and Julianne A. French, a registered nurse who I guess had big balls enough to send it to me to my home and state that I was flagged. It also states in this letter this Behavioral PRF has been entered into my medical records.

Most people would say this is unbelievable. Well, if you knew people like I do, you would probably throw up. I am inserting Julianne French's—who is retired now after she did all the trouble she could not only to me but others—Behavioral Patient Record Flag Letter, Donna Wilson's letter, and Jennifer S. Gutowski's letter.

Southern Arizona VA Health Care System
3601 S. 6th Avenue
Tucson, AZ 85723

Mr./Ms. MICHAEL R FRENCH
220 N SUNSET CIR
CASA GRANDE, ARIZONA 85122

Dear Mr./Ms. MICHAEL R FRENCH;

Providing an environment that is safe for patients, visitors, and employees is a critical factor in health care. The safety of patients and staff, as well as the effectiveness of care and patients' right to privacy and dignity, need not be compromised by safety risks. In order to ensure safety measures are maintained, there are instances when a Patient Record Flag (PRF) is entered into a patient's medical record. This PRF alerts a staff member to serious safety risks.

Please be advised that a Behavioral PRF has been entered into your medical record.

We are required by VHA Directive 2010-053 to notify a patient in writing whenever a PRF has been entered into his or her medical record. This notification to you not only ensures you are aware that a PRF has been entered into your medical record, it also provides you with the process for requesting an amendment to the presence of this PRF.

If you wish to request an amendment to this PRF in your record, you must contact the facility Privacy Officer in writing at the following address:

Southern Arizona Veterans Affairs Healthcare System (SAVAHCS)
Attn: Privacy Officer 11-136-PO
3601 S. 6th Avenue
Tucson, AZ 85723

All other inquiries about Patient Record Flags should be addressed with your SAVAHCS provider.

Sincerely,

12-6-2015

JULIANNE A FRENCH, RN
AA/COS

175

DEPARTMENT OF VETERANS AFFAIRS *checked*
Southern Arizona VA Health Care System
Tucson, AZ 85723

In Reply Refer To: 0-001-PO

November 23, 2015

Michael R. French
220 N. Sunset Cir.
Casa Grande, AZ 85122

Dear Mr. French:

This letter is in response to your amendment request submitted to the Tucson VA Medical Center on August 19, 2015 regarding information you wanted corrected in your medical record. Your request has been reviewed and processed in accordance with applicable privacy laws and regulations.

After a thorough review of your written request for an amendment and a clinical review of your records, your request has been granted in part. The physician has agreed to correct your city of residence. However, the reviewing supervisor finds that the information authored by Dr. Katherine Bonsell to be accurate, complete, and relevant in its current form. I'm enclosing a copy of the updated note for your records.

If in the future, you wish to produce further evidence that demonstrates that the clinical information is inaccurate, incomplete, or irrelevant, please submit a revised amendment request attaching all supporting documentation.

You may appeal this denial of your request for correction or amendment of your records. Your appeal will be processed pursuant to the Privacy Act standards, which require that VA maintain all records that it uses in making any determination about you with such accuracy, relevance, timeliness, and completeness as is reasonably necessary to assure fairness to you. If you choose to file an appeal, please write a letter that clearly indicates why you disagree with this initial denial with specific attention to one of more of the above four standards. Please enclose a copy of this letter with your appeal as well as any supporting documentation that demonstrates why you believe that the clinical information does not meet these requirements. Your appeal must be written, signed, and mailed to:

> Office of General Counsel (024)
> Department of Veterans Affairs
> 810 Vermont Avenue, N.W.
> Washington, D.C. 20420

If you should choose to file an appeal, please include a copy of this letter with your appeal and clearly indicate why you disagree with our determination.

If you do not choose to file an appeal, you may request the VA Medical Center provide a copy of your initial request for amendment and the denial with all future disclosures of information. You may also provide a statement of disagreement to the facility and we will include that with all future disclosures of the disputed information.

This request should be submitted in writing to me:

Donna L. Wilson, Privacy Officer
SAVAHCS
3601 S. 6th Avenue
Tucson, AZ 85723

If you deem necessary, you may submit a complaint regarding your amendment request to the VHA Privacy Office (19F), 810 Vermont Ave NW, Washington, DC 20420 or to the Secretary of the Department of Health and Human Services at (800) 368-1019.

Sincerely,

Donna L. Wilson

Donna L. Wilson, MS, CAGS, PhD(abd)
Privacy Officer

enclosure

DEPARTMENT OF VETERANS AFFAIRS
Southern Arizona VA Health Care System
Tucson, AZ 85723

FEB 0 8 2016

In Reply Refer To: 678/0-001PO

Honorable Ann Kirkpatrick
U.S. Hours of Representatives
211 North Florence St., Suite 1
Casa Grande, AZ 85122
Attn: Palmer Miller

Dear Congresswoman Kirkpatrick:

Thank you for your inquiry dated January 5, 2016 regarding Mr. Michael French and his health care concerns at the Southern Arizona VA Health Care System (SAVAHCS). I have asked Ms. Donna Wilson, Privacy Officer, and Ms. Julianne French, Administrative Assistant to the Chief of Staff, to review these concerns.

Mr. French initially contacted Ms. Wilson on August 19, 2015, regarding a record amendment to correct inaccurate information in his medical record. Attached is Ms. Wilson's response letter to Mr. French outlining the course of her investigation, the direct feedback from the provider involved, and the reason for denying the amendment request. At the conclusion of the letter is detailed information to appeal this decision.

The Patient Record Flag (PRF) on Mr. French's record was entered in response to threatening statements made by Mr. French to SAVAHCS staff. Hospitals are one of the most high-risk areas for violence and the VA has taken steps nationwide to reduce the chance of violence by developing behavioral flags to warn staff of a potentially violent patient who may pose a risk to other patients and staff. Mr. French's case was presented to the Disruptive Behavior Committee which recommended that Mr. French's electronic medical record be flagged after he stated to a staff member he would come down to the VA with "guns blazing". The VA is obligated to provide a safe environment for patients and staff. The VA will continue to monitor Mr. French's behavior and review his case again in two years. If Mr. French has no further behavioral issues, it is likely the behavioral flag will be removed at that time.

All required documents are loaded in Mr. French's record that supports he was in Camp LeJeune. He is currently being followed by his Primary Care Physician, Dr. Stephen Neustat who refers him to specialists, as necessary. If he has specific questions or concerns regarding care related to his chemical exposure, he should contact his primary care team in the Ocotillo Clinic. Additionally, if he is receiving bills for services for any of his conditions he should contact the Billing department at (520) 792-1450, extension 5487.

Lastly, in accordance with current VA policy, Mr. French is only eligible to obtain care through the Choice program when the VA cannot meet the 30-day timeliness regulations or the VA is unable to provide the needed care.

The Southern Arizona VA Health Care System strives to provide quality and compassionate care to all of our Veterans. We are very concerned with patient care and the satisfaction of the Veterans we serve. If you have further questions or concerns about this letter, please contact Donna Wilson at (520) 792-1450, extension 4347 or Julianne French at (520) 792-1450 extension 1815.

Jennifer S. Gutowski, MHA, FACHE
Acting Director
Southern Arizona
VA Health Care System

After all of these lies, Kirkpatrick's office got a hold of me, a guy that was *supposed* to help me, Palmer Miller. He said they cannot do anything for me about this matter and gave me Gutowski's letter. He then said that if I have anything else besides this incident to let him know and he would try to help me.

I laughed right in his face. I wasted all of my time with this idiot. Oh, I forgot to mention this is when Ann Kirkpatrick was running for office. I *wonder* if that is the reason why she did not want to rock the boat. She was thinking about her campaign and her political buddies. So don't listen to the lies. You better examine everything that is told to you. Like my mother told me, don't believe anything of what you hear and only half of what you see.

24

Unbelievable
So Evil

For all my readers, beware. Veterans, mothers of veterans, dads of veterans, veterans of veterans, sisters of veterans, brothers of veterans—be on the alert. They will not do one damn thing for you, and if you rock the boat as I did and call the Secretary of Veterans Affairs, Chief of Staff, or anybody of the sort, they are going to hate your guts. They will surely cut you off of everything and try to discriminate you in any way possible. The only thing they want to do is keep things running their way.

They get kickbacks just like Phoenix did in 2013 when I first moved here. In January of 2016, I called Katherine Mitchell, who was a nurse in the Phoenix VA, also the main whistleblower against Phoenix VA in 2013. They had to hush her up in a hurry. I called and spoke with her on several occasions and recorded the phone call, by the way. Katherine was basically forced to sign a gag order, which meant she traded her rights to expose these corrupt people, but in return, she got a big cushy job at the regional office and a big payoff. At least she was honest to me.

All because of the flag on my record, Nicole in Special Procedures Unit called about my colonoscopy on February 11, 2016, which I saved on my telephone. She says, "Hi, this message is for Michael French. This is Nicole. I'm calling from the Tucson VA. You have an appointment scheduled with us on February 26 at 10:30, 11:00, and 11:30. We have to cancel that. We do not have a doctor available that day. To reschedule, please give us a call. The number is 520-792-1450 extension 4747 (dog bark). Again, your appointment on February 26 at the VA hospital has been canceled. Thank you."

And I could not reschedule. I could not go to the VA or I would be arrested. But besides that, no doctors available? I don't know if I can take anymore denials from these people. But I guess I am going to have to. I have still, to this day, been bleeding from the rectum dark blood and light red blood. After wiping from one stool, I use at least a half a roll of toilet paper before the blood stops coming out.

On March 2, 2016, I got a call from Kat in Nuclear Medicine for my heart stress test. Now Dr. Neustat was setting this up for me or he said he was. He knew my heart was bothering me. This was before the flag. So I spoke with Dr. Walsh on May 22, 2015, about my stress test. I asked him if the nuclear medicine would hurt me, being that I had toxic water poisoning. He said he didn't know. He would check and I would be notified. He said he did not think that it would, that he didn't know for sure.

I was afraid to call the VA anymore. So on the date of March 2, 2016, Kat said on my voicemail on my phone, "This is Kat at the Tucson VA in Nuclear Medicine calling you back regarding whether you had a cardiac test ordered? Uh, you do not have any order for cardiac stress tests. Thank you. Any questions, call us back 520-629-1832. Bye-bye."

Knowing that I needed medical attention and fast, I did not know where to turn. Stephanie reminded me about a commercial on television called the Wounded Warrior Project. That night, I saw the commercial myself on television. I started to feel really happy because the country star, Trace Adkins, was singing his song on there. The name of the song was "Till the Last Shot's Fired." I was really excited because a verse in his song talked about in the fields of Vietnam and on the mountains of Afghanistan. Trace Adkins, in this commercial, was asking for donations for the heroes of this country, and he talked about how Wounded Warrior Project helped all the vets from PTSD to lost limbs and so on.

I got so excited I was sure that they would help me. Stephanie wrote down the number for me. There were two different numbers, 800-859-4548 and 888-962-8700. I was really excited because Trace Adkins said that the Wounded Warrior Project helped all warriors and called them his heroes. I felt very relieved that someone out there really cared. I also felt really proud for Trace Adkins that they called number one in country music was speaking for the Wounded Warrior Project. Now this commercial was asking for donations, nineteen dollars a month, monthly through your credit card.

I knew some vets that had family members get killed in the Vietnam war, and they were sending money into this organization because Trace Adkins' song, "Till the Last Shot's Fired," mentioned Vietnam. That was the era that I was in the Marine Corps. I was for certain that they wouldn't let me down or Trace Adkins.

A couple days later, I gave them a call. They started asking for my name and my credit card. I said, "First of all, I don't mind donating, but I need help myself. Who can I talk to about that?"

She said, "I could give you a number to call, but none of the donations or help from our organization will go to any branch of military or anybody in the military that was in the service post 9/11."

I then asked her what she meant. She explained to me that they don't take care of anybody before 9/11. I could not believe what I was hearing. I was tape recording this whole conversation. And I asked her, "Why then is Trace Adkins playing his song on your commercial about the Vietnam vets?"

She said she did not know. I asked for a phone number to her corporate office. This upset me in the worst way. Within the next couple weeks, I called six more times and tape recorded it. The same thing was said to me. I complained so much and so many times about Trace Adkins' song being played and explained to them that it was false advertising. And it was a low-down way to get people to send in money on a monthly basis, mind you. And then after all of my complaining, about a month later, that song was not played on the commercials anymore. But the Wounded Warrior Project states to send in money for the warriors who defended our country and the heroes. They will not tell you on television up front that the Vietnam vets, the Korean vets, WWII vets will get a penny of that money or any help at all. They are using the American veterans to rake in cash. They are betraying America.

In my opinion, they need to be audited and be accountable for every penny that is taken in by them. I let my friend listen to this recording. He had been paying in about eight months. But he stopped it right away. And I am really—*and I mean really*—*ashamed of Trace Adkins for using his song to suck in all of this money and knowing all along that his song misrepresented what was really going on.* I turned my back on him. Fraud does not sit right in my book.

In the Bible:

> For the love of money is a root of all kinds of evil. Some people, eager for money, have wandered from the faith and pierced themselves with many griefs. (1 Timothy 6:10 NIV)

25

Don't Believe Anything You Hear and Only Half of What You See

After receiving the flag and reading all of the lies that they told about me, I reviewed all of my tapes and my videos. I made my mind up that I would not step foot on that property unless I got a letter in the mail lifting the flag off of me and a formal apology. But I was told by Larry Hoth, who worked with the Chief of Staff, that what I asked for was not going to happen. I was told from time and time again that my medications slowly would decrease and then be stopped.

So on December 19, 2016, this is very much needed to be told. This would have been a conclusion to the plot. Dr. Honory, my psychiatrist, and Vicki Hervert, his nurse, persisted in coaxing me to the VA when time and time again, I told them I couldn't come or I would be arrested because of the flag. He in turn said he had to stop my medication. On recorded conversations, this went on about three months. And I was confronted with both of these people on the phone and again recorded the conversations.

They tried their best to get me to come to the parking lot and meet them. How can you have a doctor's appointment in the parking lot? I knew what they were up to. I don't know what they had in mind, but I was told by the campus police that I wasn't supposed to show up there or I would be arrested. To me, it sounded like they were trying to set me up. Then they could probably throw another psychotic label on me or something. They finally stopped calling after several calls to the chief of staff's office that I made and explained my situation which they already knew. But they also informed them that there would be a harassment charge next time they called because the chief of staff was behind this, taunting me and everything else under the definition of the word. Just like Susan MacDonald, which is very easy to prove with the reports from the police officers, my phone recordings with the dates, times, and years, and their phone records.

Now you have to remember that dealing with people like this, they have their little morning meetings, and they speak of what has to be done, what should be done, and what they are going to do. And it's not only me. I have spoken with several other vets that things of this nature have been done to. I have gotten statements from them and recordings. I had it in my mind, heart, body, and soul that these people had to be exposed. So I turned to the news media and not the fake news media. I tried to get a hold of Jeanine Pirro in New York who handled the Phoenix VA scandal with the whistleblower, Katherine Mitchell. I had no luck. So I contacted my local newspaper, *Casa Grande Dispatch*.

I spoke with a journalist at the paper. His name was Kevin Reagan. He came to my home. I proceeded telling him the story about the Tucson VA. He watched my videos and listened to my recordings. He could not believe what was going on there. He told me that he had heard from other people about things of this nature. But the other people did not go into details or have evidence like I did. After about a two-hour meeting with him in my home. He left and said he would contact me. Much to my surprise, the very next week, he had printed my story in the paper. This is one man, Kevin, who honorably honored me. Here is what he printed:

CG Veteran Afraid to Get Treated after Being "Flagged" by VA Says Recorded Comment Was "Figure of Speech"

- By Kevin Reagan, Staff Writer.
- July 9, 2017. Updated July 17, 2017.

CASA GRANDE—Michael French says he hasn't seen his doctor at the Southern Arizona VA Health Care System in over a year.

The Marine veteran suffers from multiple medical problems and wants more than anything to be treated by his doctor. But he's scared to set foot in the Tucson facility after the VA flagged him as a potential security risk.

He's not sure what may happen if he does; Veterans Affairs could say he's being a disturbance and have him arrested or detained, French claims.

The 61-year-old Casa Grande resident says the flagging was unjustified and wants to get it lifted before he returns to the Tucson hospital. Until that day comes, he'll rely on his caregiver to go to the facility to pick up his medication with his ID.

He claims the situation stemmed from a phone call he had with his doctor's nurse back in 2015.

French recorded the conversation, which he's been doing with all his phone conversations with VA personnel. He said it's a habit from his days doing law enforcement.

French shared the phone recording with PinalCentral. The conversation began with French seeking a refill of his Vicodin prescription. Then the two discussed setting up French's next appointment.

"I'm coming wide open, both barrels blazing," French said during the phone call. "This is...all this stuff has got to come to an end right now."

French said this statement was a figure of speech, meant to convey his eagerness to see his doctor again. But it appears VA staff interpreted the statement differently.

In documents shared with PinalCentral, the nurse recorded notes of the conversation with French. She recalled him being "very upset" and stated he was coming down to the facility with "guns blazing."

French insists his statement was not a threat. Yet, a couple months after the phone call, he received a letter notifying him a behavioral flag had been entered into his medical record.

It is VA policy to flag a patient's health record if he or she is seen as an immediate threat to self or others. The presence of a flag is not meant to refuse services to patients, according to the agency's policy, as it's meant to inform medical staff of a patient's behavioral problems.

In 2013, the VA Office of Inspector General released a report critiquing how the agency flags patients. One issue identified by inspectors was that the VA facilities had inconsistent definitions of "disruptive behavior," thus potentially creating disunity in how patients were flagged.

In an email, the national VA office said it has addressed the recommendations made in the OIG report. It has defined disruptive behavior as "whether its occurrence would create fear in a reasonable person."

The OIG recently visited the Tucson VA and reviewed how it manages disruptive patients. No recommendations were listed in the inspector's March report regarding patient flags, aside from a directive to have all employees undergo disruptive behavior training within 90 days of hire.

The Tucson VA told PinalCentral patient-privacy rules barred the VA from discussing French's situation.

But a spokesman for the facility said it does not turn away veterans seeking medical treatment, and it wouldn't restrict access to those who have their medical files flagged.

Flagged patients who have questions or concerns are encouraged to contact a patient advocate, the spokesman added.

French said he contacted a patient advocate at the Tucson VA shortly after being flagged and claims that didn't help.

In April, French recorded a conversation with his doctor, who repeatedly told French he needed to come in and be evaluated. But French reminded him there was a flag on his file.

"I'm scared to go down there," he told PinalCentral, "I don't know what they're going to do to me."

On Monday, French spoke with a VA administrator who informed him of a pending review of his case before the discipline committee that flags patients. French said he was glad to know somebody cares about his situation.

Despite this revelation, French is still on a mission to clear his name of wrongdoing. He's skeptical the issue will be resolved so he's taking VA staff to small claims court for outside medical costs he's incurred while not receiving treatment.

French said he's not doing it for the money; he wants the VA to admit it was wrong so his credibility can be restored.

With his long white hair and arms covered in tattoos, French looks quite different from the 17-year-old who enlisted in the Marines more than 40 years ago.

During the Vietnam War, his draft number was called, and French was expecting to enlist in the Army. He chose to enlist in a delayed-entry program in which he'd go out and recruit others to join the Marines—even before he was a Marine.

French started boot camp at Parris Island in South Carolina and claims he was the victim of physical and mental abuse at the hands of his drill instructor.

During the 1970s, French spent some time stationed at Camp Lejeune in North Carolina working as a driver. He believes this is where he was contaminated with toxins that later made him sick.

Wells at the camp were shut down in 1985 after the drinking water was found to be contaminated with industrial chemicals. The exact duration and intensity of the contamination is unknown, according to the VA, but the agency says those who lived at the camp between 1953 and 1985 are most at risk.

Studies done by the Agency for Toxic Substances and Disease Registry concluded those exposed to the water are at an increased risk for cancer and other adverse health effects.

The VA began accepting disability claims this year for veterans exposed to chemicals in Lejeune's water.

French first encountered a problem in 1989 after a doctor discovered nine cancerous polyps in his body. They were removed but that didn't end his health hiccups.

One day he noticed he was talking like Vito Corleone from the "The Godfather" and more cancer was removed from his throat. He began experiencing spouts of vertigo, had troubles with his bladder and was later diagnosed with post-traumatic stress disorder.

It's all resulted in him being given a long list of medications he now relies on.

French decided to move to Casa Grande after he heard the VA hospitals in Arizona could treat veterans sickened by the water contamination at Camp Lejeune. Unfortunately, he said, he's been disappointed by the care he's gotten.

Throughout his home, French has hallmarks on display from his life before Arizona: certificates earned while in the Marines and pictures of him during his guitar-playing musician days.

The VA staff probably didn't like him always recording and documenting conversations, French said, which is why he feels they tried to push him out by flagging him as a threat.

He claims to have called at least 17 other VA facilities in the country, but because the flag system is universal within the agency, he said the flag will pop up wherever he tries to go.

"I'm just at odds," French said, "I don't know what to do."

May God help me. He is. He will. Michael French. Honorably dishonored.

26

I Will Prove My Innocence; I Will

Oh, and one more thing about little Miss Susan MacDonald. Approximately springtime in 2017, I compiled all of my tape recordings and videotapes. I got all of my evidence together. Because even after all this stuff MacDonald did to me, all the lies and accusations, she still persisted to call and leave messages on my phone. In return, I called an officer from the Casa Grande Police Department and explained to him that I had told her plentiful times to never call my phone again. What was she trying to prove now by calling my phone and harassing me, laughing, and giggling because I am very sick from toxic water poisoning from Camp Lejeune and being flagged for two years and not being able to go to any VA? I guess this just made her so very happy.

But the officer listened to the phone message and called her back and told her, "Never call Mr. French again or you will have a harassment charge on you."

So in turn, Stephanie and I decided to go to civil court here in Casa Grande and prove my innocence of ever making any statement about weapons, guns, or anything of the sort. There was a subpoena served on Susan right there in Ocotillo Clinic at Tucson VA on July 31, 2017.

The day we were supposed to appear in Casa Grande Civil Court was on August 23, 2017. Stephanie and I arrived at the court and were flabbergasted on what they told me. The justice court stood in for Susan. About a week later, I received two packets from the justice court saying I needed to get a lawyer and appear in justice court. I did not have the funds to purchase a rightful attorney. So the case just died out. That's what they think. Yes, she is a girl and probably has hundreds of talents. Evidently, someone else thought the same thing.

My next step still is to contact Judge Jeanine Pirro. I plan on signing and dedicating one book to her and one book to our dear president, Donald J. Trump. Here are the harassment police reports and also where, somehow, she avoided civil court. But I'm not done yet. I will expose this wickedness. I will expose these wicked actions. So help me God. So I am also enclosing in my book documents, reports, letters, newspaper clippings, and anything of the sort to let you see and believe that this book is all a true story and not fiction. Although sometimes, I wish it was fiction. I don't know how much more I can take. God bless all of you.

```
7/19/16                    SunGard CAD                        PAGE   1
8:28:15                 CAD CALL INFORMATION                  162000174
```

```
Call Number: 162000174      Call Type.: 104 TELEPHONE HARASSMENT   Police
Entry Day/Tm:  7/18/16 12:02:00         108 HARASSMENT             Police

CmnN:                              Agency.........: 001 CASA GRANDE POLIC
Location...:                                    CIR   Apt:
City......:  CASA GRANDE    Block#:    200   Loc ID:  Mapr: B6
Intersectn.: PARKVIEW                    DEAD END

Caller Name: L: FRENCH                  F: MICHAEL         M:
Address...:                                          Apt:
City/State:                                          Source: 8700

Call Taker.:      9197 MCCOY            KELLY          QPADEV000N
Dispatcher.:      9152 TORRES          FIDEL          QPADEV000C
```

```
              N A R R A T I V E

***** 21 traffic *****                              12:02:39
wants to report a 101 in tucson keeps harrassing him   12:02:58
by calling                                          12:03:01

Call change from 415P to 415T BY QPADEV000N P 01 0000009197   12:03:03

#9, spoke w/RP told me that his Dr. Off. Dr.Neustat/susan   14:11:03
mcdonald keeps calling from the VA and harass. him via   14:11:03
phone. told me that he spoke with the office back in sep   14:11:03
2015 and told the office not to call. i asked what kind of   14:11:03
Harass. he told me that the last call was 7/18/16 at 1047   14:11:03
hrs left msg of: this susan returning your phone call. i   14:11:03
adv  RP told me that he has a lawyer with fuller &   14:11:03
stowell. i asked him why his lawyers is not sending a   14:11:03
letter to the Dr's offi. told me that they are collecting   14:11:03
information and that he wanted to document the phone call.   14:11:03
advise Rp that this sounds like a civil issue. i gave RP a   14:11:03
curtsey call and to the office.i made contact with Susan   14:11:03
who adv me that RP called them and thats why she is   14:11:03
returning his phone call. Susan adv that someone from the   14:11:03
VA will call Rp. I called RP and adv that someone will   14:11:03
call from the VA. Rp was satisfied  that he will recieve a   14:11:03
call.                                               14:11:03
```

```
*NONE              Unit Status History Information

7/18/16 12:02:00  18 Route Call Time      RT   |


287                Unit Status History Information

7/18/16 12:03:32   4 Dispatched          D    |    287 MORA,AAR
7/18/16 12:03:32  11 Assigned as Primary  PR   |
7/18/16 12:09:16  16 Reset Unit Time Chec RS   |
7/18/16 12:09:41   9 Started Self-Initiat SC M |
7/18/16 12:19:10  10 Ended Self-Initiated EC   |
7/18/16 12:19:12   9 Started Self-Initiat SC   |
```

Pinal County Justice Courts, Arizona

Casa Grande Justice Court   820 E Cottonwood Ln Bldg B Casa Grande AZ 85122 (520)-836-5471

CASE NUMBER: C V 201700/081

Plaintiff(s): MICHAEL FRENCH
CASA GRANDE, AZ 85123
( ) -
Plaintiff(s) Name / Address / Phone

Defendant(s): SUSAN MACDONALD
Defendant(s) Name / Address / Phone

( ) -
Attorney for Plaintiff(s) Name / Address / Phone

( ) -
Attorney for Defendant(s) Name / Address / Phone

APPLICATION FOR ENTRY OF DEFAULT
JCRCP Rule 140

I am the ☒ Plaintiff ☐ Counterclaimant ☐ 3rd Party Plaintiff ☐ Attorney

THE FOLLOWING WERE SERVED THE SUMMONS AND COMPLAINT:

Defendant(s): _PLACe of woRk_

NOTICE to Defendant(s):
If you do not answer or file a responsive pleading with the court within ten (10) judicial days of the filing of this Application, the Default will be effective and the Party may request a Judgment to be entered against you.

I am applying for an Entry of Default against the above named party who has failed to timely file a response to the lawsuit.

The Defendant was served the Summons and Complaint by:

☒ Process Server   ☐ Alternative Service
☐ Publication   ☐ Certified Mail *(Small Claims)*

The Defendant ☐ is ☒ is not on active duty in the United States Military.

Date: 8- -2017   Signature _Michael French_
☒ Plaintiff ☐ Counterclaimant ☐ 3rd Party Plaintiff ☐ Attorney

NOTICE to PARTY filing for Default:
Any time after ten (10) judicial days have passed since the filing of this Application, it is your responsibility to file a Request for Entry of Default Judgment or request a hearing. A Statement of Costs and proof of the claim (receipts, contract, etc.) must also be served upon all the parties in this lawsuit.

I CERTIFY that a copy of this document has been or will be mailed on _8-23-2017_ to:

☐ Plaintiff at the above address ☐ Plaintiff's attorney ☒ Defendant at the above address ☐ Defendant's attorney

Date: _AUG 23, 2017_   By _Michael French_
Signature

R: 1/20/15

198

Pinal County Justice Courts, Arizona

Casa Grande Justice Court   820 E Cottonwood Ln Bldg B Casa Grande AZ 85122 (520)-836-5471

CASE NUMBER: CV 201700108l

MICHAEL FRENCH

CASA GRANDE, AZ. 85122

( )   -

Plaintiff(s) Name / Address / Phone

SUSAN MAC DONALD

( )   -

Defendant(s) Name / Address / Phone

( )   -

Attorney for Plaintiff(s) Name / Address / Phone

( )   -

Attorney for Defendant(s) Name / Address / Phone

REQUEST and AFFIDAVIT FOR ENTRY OF DEFAULT JUDGMENT
☒ With Hearing   ☐ Without Hearing   JCRCP Rule 140

I request that the Court enter a default judgment.

If I am the Plaintiff, then I state that the Summons, Complaint and the Notice to Defendant were served on the Defendant. No response has been received within the time allowed by law. At least ten (10) judicial days have passed since the Entry of Default.

The Defendant ☐ is ☒ is not on active duty in the United States Military.

Principal $	3,500
Costs $	8,680.04
Attorney fees $	1,217 99/100
Interest $	
Total $	13,398.03

Attached are the: ☐ Proposed Judgment
☐ Supporting documents / proof of debt
☐ Statement of cost

I state under penalty of perjury that the forgoing is true and correct.

Date: 8-23-2017   Signature _____

☐ Plaintiff ☐ Counterclaimant ☐ 3rd Party Plaintiff ☐ Attorney

Note: *A party who files a proposed default judgment must also provide the court with stamped envelopes addressed to each party.*

I CERTIFY that a copy of this document has been or will be mailed on 8-23-2017 to:

☐ Plaintiff at the above address   ☐ Plaintiff's attorney   ☒ Defendant at the above address   ☐ Defendant's attorney

Date: 8-23-2017   By _____
Signature

R: 1/20/16

199

27

Digging Deep into Our Government for Help?

I have been seeking and searching every avenue to set things right, to find a truthful person who has the fear of God in him or her. I have found some great honorable people who honored me, like the police officers and the writer at the newspaper. I just feel sorry for the vets that I have talked to that were treated in this fashion and were done wrong. I don't understand how they could just forget things like this and go through life. Or maybe they don't forget these things that the VA has done to them.

I know it has to eat at them straight to the bone. I want to tell them all right now or anybody that is done wrong in any way. I want to tell all of you just what my mother told me. She said, "Mike, you don't have to take these things. Stand up for yourself. But do it in a Godly way." Thanks, Mom.

All through the year of 2017 to the beginning of 2018, I called Secretary of Veterans Affairs. Bob McComber is who I spoke to. He told me how to fill out a complaint and get a case number. He also gave me a number of David

Schulkin who was the head of the office. David Schulkin would never answer or return my calls.

So then I called and started originating cases with the Veterans Integrated Network also known as the Whitehouse VA Hotline, and the team members told me that David Schulkin never talked to anyone that had a complaint.

Well, that blew my mind because I thought that was his job. Who is paying wrongly for someone to have a job when they are not doing that job? My guess is the taxpayers. I had four case numbers—14500, 17620, 18312, and 23055. The team members I spoke to on different occasions were Lori, Ryan, Jessica, Connie, Alex, Will, James, Rodney, Leslie, Mary, Janice, and Mark, a supervisor. I also spoke to Steven who was in the Inspector General office. Each one of the members told me to call back every two weeks, and nothing ever happened.

I, Michael French, declare that I admire, respect, look up to, and am happy for our new president, Donald J. Trump. I know for a fact I saw him on television speaking about the Choice Program and what he would do about firing doctors, staff, or whoever that did not enforce what his speech was concerning, and that was to make sure that the VAs, the hospitals, would send vets out into the community for treatment if they could not or would not treat the vets. All through my book, I have proof from recordings that I made, videotapes, and messages on my phone, that I was one of many that the staff of the VAs had disobeyed President Trump's orders. I saw him on television making these statements. Whenever and whoever I spoke with and quoted President Trump's orders to at the Tucson VA hospital, they laughed very smugly. That tells me they did not only disrespect me as a vet that served for our country and many others, but *they disrespected my president,* Donald J. Trump! I am sorry for them, my president.

28

Things Are Going to Get Better

I refuse to let them get me down. I know God has got a plan for me, and it is not here in Arizona. Stephanie and I discuss all of the time about getting married. We have a platonic relationship. So therefore, with respect to Father God, the Son, and the Holy Spirit, we want God to bless our marriage when we do get married. We went to Zales and picked out her engagement rings and both comfort fit wedding bands. So now it is official. We are engaged. Planning to move back to Chicago and finding a home is going to be a big job by itself. We have to sell this house, and that is going to be a big job in itself also. But all of the work that we put into this house I know everyone is going to want it. And for the right price, someone can buy it.

We built a twelve-foot-wide and six-foot-tall waterfall for our pool. We built it out of boulders, flagstone, and fabricated rock. We put a fiberglass alligator at the top of the mountain, and it really looks real. The alligator sits on a flat rock. It's about four feet long, and the water shoots out about six inches underneath the alligator through the rock. You can control the amount of water on the pump.

This saltwater pool also has built-in lights and jets by the steps where you step down into the pool. I found this to be very relaxing for my back. I also built a koi pond with a waterfall on the other side of the redwood deck we built with a pergola. We have bamboo all on the walls around the backyard and an indoor/outdoor bar area with an indoor electric smoker, popcorn machine, and television. That is just some of the features that are going to be sold with the house. We did a great job on this house, but this is not home. We are both from the Midwest, and we miss the Christmas spirit and the four seasons and the snow. Face it, you cannot decorate a cactus for Christmas. It turns into a real sticky situation.

So now we are preparing and getting a mindset to move and get out of here. I know that Hines VA hospital in Chicago is a good hospital. I have all of this moving to think about. Traveling back across country about two thousand miles, selling one house, buying another. And with all of these things wrong with me, it really drains me, my mind and body. I know God is the only reason, besides Stephanie, that keeps me going. Most of the time, I have to use a cane for my right ankle. But when I use the cane with my right wrist, it starts to hurt because of the carpal tunnel. I have gout arthritis all over my body.

I don't want to bore you with my complaints and my body aches, but I am in pain as I am writing right now. I don't know what I would do without pain. It has become part of me. As long as I can keep my head up and think positive thoughts, I will deal with it. On the other hand, I am a writer. It first started with music. I have four hundred and twenty-six songs that I have written myself of which two of the songs I gave Gary Loizzo credit for co-writing. He was a front man and lead singer for the group American Breed. He was also the founder and owner of Pumpkin Recording Studio in Orland Park, Illinois.

I looked up to Gary. He recorded my songs at Pumpkin and sang backup vocals for me. He also helped me rearrange some of my material. His son, Todd Loizzo, also helped out with digital drum tracks and keyboards on some of the songs. We did thirteen together with full band tracks. This was all analog and sounds great. Then I came back and recorded ten acoustic tracks, just me and my guitar. Like I said, I try to be positive in life, and this song material is also a reflection of my life. With all of the stress that I have been going through, I have to be goofy sometimes to try to forget about it.

So Stephanie and I decided to write standup comedy skits. We changed our names for the comedy. Stephanie would be Squeak, and I myself would be Homer Shagnasty. Homer speaks with a harelip, and when he first comes out on stage, he says, "Hey! I tell you one damn thing! And when I think of something else, I'll tell you that too!"

So with this being said regarding the VA, I have already thought of something else, and now I am going to tell them too. Like I said before, I don't know how the other poor vets I have talked to go through life with their heads down. They fought for our country. They fought for you and me. I don't understand how the VA hospitals can mistreat them and push them down to the ground like they are nobody like they are dirt; like they are meaningless. I bet the directors in the hospital don't think about themselves or their families or their friends as being protected by these poor vets. They forget about all of that.

Remember to watch the full-length movie titled *Article 99* because if you watch this movie, you will see what I myself and so many other veterans are going through every day. I do respectfully feel that our president, Donald Trump, would not tolerate these ordeals if he knew what was going on. If he needs evidence, *I have it*. I have been getting calls here lately from Larry Hoth at the Tucson VA asking me to come back. I explained to him like a hundred other times that I would not set foot on that property unless I had a written letter from the chief of staff's office and Director that my flag no longer existed.

29

Has My Persistence Paid Off? Let's See.

After all of my calling Washington and complaining, after all of the newspaper reports trying to bring their wrongdoings to the surface, and after all of this time since 2013 with no treatment except for *pills*, I feel the ground moving. I am totally worn-out and waking up every day to only worry about which way I am going to turn for medical treatment—operations, procedures, and so forth.

I guess, in fact, Washington had questioned the Tucson VA about their ethics and the way they treated the patients. Larry called me around the first week of September 2017 and told me that the flag was lifted. I demanded a letter to be sent to me, and it was. I received it in the mail a couple days later. So here is the letter that I received.

Southern Arizona VA Health Care System
3601 S. 6th Avenue
Tucson, AZ 85723

Mr. MICHAEL .. FRENCH

Dear Mr. MICHAEL R FRENCH:

Please be advised that the Behavioral Cat I Patient Record Flag (PRF)was
recently reviewed. The outcome was to remove the flag from your medical
record.

The Behavior PRF was removed as per review.

Sincerely,

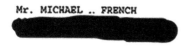

Lawrence R. Hoth RN, BSN, DC
AO Chief of Staff

So in late August 2017, when the flag was finally lifted, Larry Hoth in the Tucson VA Chief of Staff's office called me and said the investigation form had showed up finally. He wanted to fill it out over the phone with me, so as I recorded the phone call, I answered the questions he asked me, and I asked him after the questioning was over, "Could, in fact, the chief of staff's office just bury this and it could go nowhere then?"

He chuckled a bit and said, "Absolutely."

On August 30, 2017, I had an appointment set up to see Dr. Neustat. I was so nervous. I called the VA police and explained to them my flag was lifted, but I wanted them at my appointment. I knew Susan MacDonald still worked with Dr. Neustat, and I did not know what she was capable of. Larry Hoth said he would be at the appointment also.

When I arrived at the Ocotillo Clinic at the Tucson VA, there was an officer for me on my behalf. But Larry Hoth was not there like he promised, but there was a guy by the name of Bob Klein. He was an AOD. He explained to me that Larry could not be there, and he was standing in for him. I waited for an hour and a half. I asked them, "What is going on? Why can't I see the doctor?"

They said he was called out on an emergency. This was all looking very weird, and I was feeling very uneasy about the whole thing. So I told Bob Klein and the officer that I had to leave and would call back and set up another appointment. Klein kept saying, "Stay, stay, stay."

I said, "I am gone." Stephanie and I got into our car and started heading back to Casa Grande. Halfway home, I got a call from Dr. Neustat. He wanted me to turn around and come back. I told him, "No way! I'm in pain and I'm already over half of the way home." There was tons of traffic out, and I did not feel like driving back through it. So we came to an agreement and set the appointment for September 7, 2017.

My ankle proceeded to swell, and I could not put any pressure on it at all. They told me in Orthopedics that when I broke my toe, it shattered into my ankle. Dr. Jabczenski didn't do anything for me. This was in 2015. So September 6, I had to go to the Casa Grande VA Clinic for a blood test that Dr. Neustat ordered. When I arrived there, they would not give it to me at first. They said I had to have an appointment for it. After about an hour of making calls to the Tucson VA to the chief of staff's office, complaining again, the clinic decided to give me a blood test.

On the way out of the front door, the door shut right on my bad ankle. It was horrible! It rolled my ankle as it shut. So I then called the VA at the Ocotillo Clinic and explained to them that I had to reschedule tomorrow, which would be the seventh, Dr. Neustat's appointment with me. They said they would have someone call me. So on the seventh of September 2017, Tige Lewis, an AOD, called. I knew this man. He said that Dr. Neustat wasn't going to be in the office anyway on the seventh and he said my appointment was scheduled now for the fifteenth of September 2017. So I told him I was happy to hear from him and was looking forward to seeing him again and then said goodbye.

Stephanie helped me soak my leg and doctor it. It was really bad now. The swelling really wasn't going down at all.

It felt like a bone up above my ankle was going to poke out of my leg. That is where the rash was. But I had to get ready for this appointment because something had to be done with my ankle and other parts of my body. I thought for sure that everything would be all right now. But I was still nervous, so I called the VA hospital police again on the day of my appointment. I told them I wanted them there. But what I found out when I got there was that the police were told to be there anyway. I don't know who from. I'm just thinking it was a smart aleck move from Susan MacDonald. I don't know for sure. But Larry Hoth was there, and we had to go inside and wait in one room for Neustat.

When they said that we could go down to his office, he was coming out while we were going in and gave me a dirty look. That really freaked me out. Also in the room, besides Larry and Neustat, was Dr. King, my dermatologist, Dr. Lees, who I found out later wanted to be my doctor, and Cynthia, a head RN for Ocotillo Clinic. I hobbled in there with Stephanie who was wired and recording the whole incident. I got introduced to the doctors and nurses. Dr. King I already knew.

We brought our computer laptop and also played for them how I was treated over the phone by Rita Watson in the Emergency Room stating that I could not come because I was going to bring guns and kill everybody. They didn't have anything to say about that. I just wanted to show them some of the things I was going through. In fact, they wanted to change the subject. So I did. I proceeded with Stephanie's help to take off my shoes and socks. If you can imagine the size of an unused brand-new paper towel roll, that is what my right ankle looked like. Again, they didn't do anything about this. The dermatologist wanted to send me some cream. I don't know how this was going to absorb through my skin to my bones, but I just went along with them. The rest of them just circled around, looking at my right ankle swollen with the scab approximately eight inches long up my leg and the width of around to the front and the back. My left ankle also had a scab about the same size. I don't know to this day what caused that. But I do know that my broken toe that had splintered and shattered did something to my ankle.

Dr. Neustat personally brought me to imaging and gave me a series of X-rays on my ankle. They also wanted to X-ray my chest and my right rotator cuff. I don't know how I tore it again, but it was probably from grabbing onto things trying to maintain my balance because of my ankle. I had a tear in that right rotator cuff in 1998. But Dr. Tonino in Chicago at Loyola University performed orthoscopic surgery, and I might say he is a great, great doctor. From my understanding, he was also a doctor for the Chicago Cubs.

He repaired my rotator cuff, and in no time, it was as good as new. But now it hurts really bad. So when they took the X-rays, they saw the tear in my rotator cuff and the damage in my right ankle. So the only one that I could get an answer from about my X-rays was Dr. Lees. Here is the report:

Progress Notes

```
LOCAL TITLE: Patient Notification Letter -- Imaging
STANDARD TITLE: LETTERS
DATE OF NOTE: OCT 18, 2017@09:34      ENTRY DATE: OCT 18, 2017@09:34:19
       AUTHOR: LEES,JOHN K              EXP COSIGNER:
       URGENCY:                              STATUS: COMPLETED
```

Patient MICHAEL ● FRENCH,

This to inform you of the following test results.

Radiology/Imaging Procedure tests
Date
10/18/2017

Comments: Your recent FOOT x-rays showed :

RIGHT FOOT :

There is a great toe bunion deformity
There are "hammer toe" deformities of the second through fifth toes.

 There are mild-to-moderate degenerative findings of the great toe
 (base of the great toe)

  Impression:
  1. There is increased density in the calcaneal body
  (heel, at base of ankle) which may be related to injury
  2. Degenerative findings include involvement of the 'forefoot'

LEFT FOOT :
There is a great toe bunion deformity and
"hammer toe" deformities of the second through fifth toes.

Your recent RIGHT SHOULDER x-rays showed :

 There are moderate degenerative findings of the acromioclavicular joint.
  (where the 'collarbone' meets the shoulder

      Impression:
       AC joint degenerative findings.

Search the MEDICAL LIBRARY at www.MyHealth.va.gov under Healthwise for
more test information.

If you have any questions or concerns please contact your PACT team:
Ocotillo: 520-629-4881

PATIENT NAME ▓▓▓▓▓▓▓▓▓▓
FRENCH, MICHAEL ●▓▓

CASA GRANDE, ARIZONA   85122
▓▓▓▓▓▓▓▓

VISTA Electronic Medical Documentation
Printed at SOUTHERN ARIZONA VA HCS

Page 1

Now you see on Dr. Lees's notes, he also talks about the bunions on my toes. I have also repeatedly asked Dr. Neustat and Dr. Jabczenski to address my issues. I was supposed to have this operation done at the Nashville VA in Tennessee before I left to Arizona, but I decided to wait until I got to Arizona because of the time period that I needed for healing after the operation.

So my podiatrist—his name was Timothy J. Byron DPM, MS with the Podiatrist Group Incorporated, Diplomate, American Board of Podiatric Surgery, Fellow American College of Foot and Ankle Surgeons, Fellow American Academy of Podiatric Sports Medicine—was a really good doctor, and I might add Dr. Lees, in my opinion, is the best primary doctor that I know. Even though he was not my doctor, he stood up for me. You can tell by the notes that he was on my side.

Here also is what Dr. Byron called my foot fix kit. He told me to carry it to any hospital that I went to and seek out a podiatrist to do this operation. I was denied this at the Tucson VA so many times I cannot count. Only Dr. Lees pointed it out about my bunions in his notes, and here is Dr. Byron's notes of my foot fix kit:

U.S. DEPARTMENT OF VETERANS AFFAIRS
VA TENNESSEE VALLEY HEALTHCARE SYSTEM

Timothy J. Byron, DPM, MS
Podiatric Surgery

1310 24th Ave. So.
Nashville, TN 37212-2637
(615) 327-4751 Ext. 68513

Telephone: (615) 873-8513
Fax: (615) 873-7901
Toll Free: (800) 228-4973 ext. 68513

After hours/weekends/holidays call (615) 327-4751 and
ask for the Surgical Officer of the Day or S.O.D.

TIMOTHY J. BYRON, D.P.M., M.S.
Podiatrist Group, Inc.
DIPLOMATE, AMERICAN BOARD OF PODIATRIC SURGERY
FELLOW, AMERICAN COLLEGE OF FOOT & ANKLE SURGEONS
FELLOW, AMERICAN ACADEMY OF PODIATRIC SPORTS MEDICINE

HALLUX ABDUCTO-VALGUS "BUNION" SURGERY
Possible Complications

Foot:
☑ Right
☐ Left
☐ Both

Anesthesia:
☑ Anesthetic & Possible Complications (Hospital)

Suture reaction:
☑ Absorbable, Threads & Screws
☑ Plastic Surgical Closure, Skin

Healing of Soft Tissue & Bone: 4WKS
☑ Vitamins & Minerals: centrum
☑ Walking Splint

Infection:
☑ Bone & Soft Tissue
☐ Around Spacer

Rejection:
☐ Spacer
☐ Silicone Synovitis

Alternatives:
☑ Do Nothing
☑ Loose soft shoe
☑ Mechanical Only
   Orthotic Devices

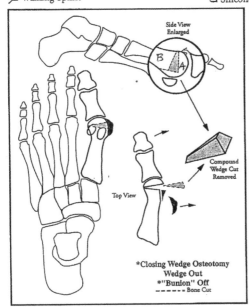

Side View
Enlarged

B A

Compound
Wedge Cut
Removed

Top View

*Closing Wedge Osteotomy
Wedge Out
*"Bunion" Off
- - - - - - Bone Cut

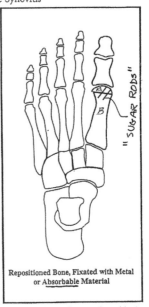

"SUGAR RODS"

Repositioned Bone, Fixated with Metal
or Absorbable Material

This worksheet is designed to assist our patient in understanding the planned procedure (s). Areas
of bony fusion or osteotomy (bone cuts), incisions, or use of hardware have been indicated.
By my signature, I acknowledge that this procedure has been fully explained to me.

X _____   _____
Patient (Guardian) Signature   Date:

8/24/99

U.S. DEPARTMENT OF VETERANS AFFAIRS
VA TENNESSEE VALLEY HEALTHCARE SYSTEM

Timothy J. Byron, DPM, MS
Podiatric Surgery

TIMOTHY J. BYRON, D.P.M., M.S.
Podiatrist Group, Inc.
DIPLOMATE, AMERICAN BOARD OF PODIATRIC SURGERY
FELLOW, AMERICAN COLLEGE OF FOOT & ANKLE SURGEONS
FELLOW, AMERICAN ACADEMY OF PODIATRIC SPORTS MEDICINE

1310 24th Ave. So.
Nashville, TN 37212-2637
(615) 327-4751 Ext. 68513

Telephone: (615) 873-8513
Fax: (615) 873-7901
Toll Free: (800) 228-4973 ext. 68513

After hours/weekends/holidays call (615) 327-4751 and
ask for the Surgical Officer of the Day or S.O.D.

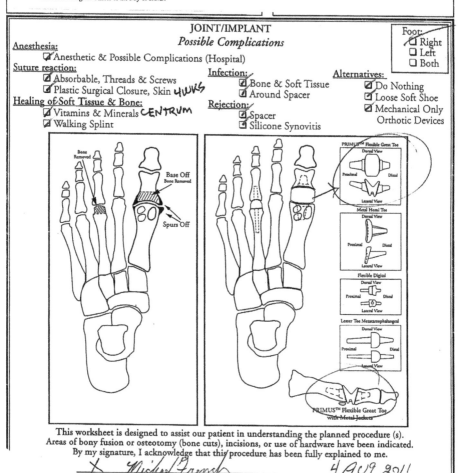

JOINT/IMPLANT
Possible Complications

Foot:
☑ Right
☐ Left
☐ Both

Anesthesia:
☑ Anesthetic & Possible Complications (Hospital)

Suture reaction:
☑ Absorbable, Threads & Screws
☑ Plastic Surgical Closure, Skin 4WKS

Healing of Soft Tissue & Bone:
☑ Vitamins & Minerals CENTRUM
☑ Walking Splint

Infection:
☑ Bone & Soft Tissue
☑ Around Spacer

Rejection:
☑ Spacer
☑ Silicone Synovitis

Alternatives:
☑ Do Nothing
☑ Loose Soft Shoe
☑ Mechanical Only
Orthotic Devices

This worksheet is designed to assist our patient in understanding the planned procedure (s).
Areas of bony fusion or osteotomy (bone cuts), incisions, or use of hardware have been indicated.
By my signature, I acknowledge that this procedure has been fully explained to me.

X _Michael French_   Date: 4 AUG 2011

Patient (Guardian) Signature

So you see, I have multiple serious problems in my body. These bunions on both feet hurt so bad they get so inflamed and along with my right ankle that needs to be operated on and my toe that was shattered and splintered into the ankle on the right foot. And my gout arthritis that I have to deal with all through my body but especially in my feet and ankles, it really makes it hard to get around. It is pretty bad when you go to a hospital and you speak with doctors that say they took the Hippocratic Oath. Let's see, there is a classic version of that oath and there is a modern version of the Hippocratic Oath. Here is the modern version by Louis Lasagna, dean of the school of medicine at Tufts University in 1964:

> I swear to fulfill, to the best of my ability and judgment, this covenant: I will respect the hard-won scientific gains of those physicians in whose steps I walk, and gladly share such knowledge as is mine with those who are to follow. I will apply, for the benefit of the sick, all measures which are required, avoiding those twin traps of overtreatment and therapeutic nihilism. I will remember that there is art to medicine as well as science, and that warmth, sympathy, and understanding may outweigh the surgeon's knife or the chemist's drug. I will not be ashamed to say "I know not," nor will I fail to call in my colleagues when the skills of another

are needed for a patient's recovery. I will respect the privacy of my patients, for their problems are not disclosed to me that the world may know. Most especially must I tread with care in matters of life and death. If it is given me to save a life, all thanks. But it may also be within my power to take a life; this awesome responsibility must be faced with great humbleness and awareness of my own frailty. Above all, I must not play at God. I will remember that I do not treat a fever chart, a cancerous growth, but a sick human being, whose illness may affect the person's family and economic stability. My responsibility includes these related problems, if I am to care adequately for the sick. I will prevent disease whenever I can, for prevention is preferable to cure. I will remember that I remain a member of society, with special obligations to all my fellow human beings, those sound of mind and body as well as the infirm. If I do not violate this oath, may I enjoy life and art, respected while I live and remembered with affection thereafter. May I always act so as to preserve the finest traditions of my calling and may I long experience the joy of healing those who seek my help.

So now I have to talk with Larry Hoth from the chief of staff's office and Dr. Neustat, my primary care doctor, about getting a doctor to operate on me. This has been going on since 2015. There have been other things that have happened. I broke a rib in my right side next to my sternum, and I think I have a high anal hernia. Because there is like a bubble in my chest when I lay down at night, I think my tissue is torn. So we will see what happens.

All this is happening for a reason and is God's plan. I know this deep in my heart. Well, after about a month or two later, I realized that this was what had been done. President Trump's slogan is "Make America Great Again," and the world as I know it right now, in the news on different channels, has people saying we have to come together. I do know this is true, and I do believe *we need to come together*. So if, in fact, there is any veteran or person that has been wrongfully done, like myself, please have your evidence ready, such as videos, recordings, paper trails, e-mails. You can contact me through my publishing company or attorneys. Let us see if we can come together.

Oh, I forgot to add this last part: compassionate and sincere. One thing I would like to leave this chapter with is in the New Testament of the Bible, New International Version, in 1 John 2:15–17:

> Do not love the world or anything in the world. If anyone loves the world, the love of the Father is not in him. For everything in the world—the cravings of sinful man, the lust of his eyes and the boasting of what he has and does-comes not from the Father but from the world. The world and its desires pass away, but the man who does the will of God lives forever.

30

Who's Got the Knife? Will I Survive?

Well, here we go. Larry Hoth and Stephen Neustat set me up to go to see Dr. Jabczenski for my operations. But if it wasn't for Dr. John Lees standing up for me, this would not have happened. So in my opinion and in my heart, Dr. Lees is honorably honored. He is a very good man and a very good doctor. He has got a brain and compassion for others. He doesn't have to say anything. You can just see it in his eyes and feel it when you are around him. He has got a light all around him. He is a great asset to any institution that he serves.

My opinion is he should have his own private practice. In Stephanie's opinion, this is what she said about him. This is Stephanie with her own words:

"The way he looked when I was telling him Michael's problems and no one giving us help for anything, he gave me a look of concern, like he was actually caring about Michael and what I said. He was the only one that showed any compassion for Michael and his medical problems. A well-dressed, well-groomed, thin but a healthy physique, and well-maintained personal appearance—black tie, white shirt, black pants, and black shoes. With his freshly cleaned white doctor's coat, he sparkled. Like Michael said, he had a white light all around him. He spoke with authority and with great knowledge."

Dr. King, the Dermatologist, was also there, and I had a growth coming out the right side of my head about the size of a peanut. I showed Dr. King while we were all in the room, and I explained to him about Nashville VA burning off precancers on my face, which they finally found on the screen only because I brought my progress notes from Nashville. Otherwise, they would not have found it. Dr. King said that he would plunge my head. I freaked out and said, "Plunge my head? What are you talking about?"

He explained that they would have to shave some of my hair and take this device and tap into my skull to pull out the core. This really sounded scary to me. Dr. Lees also shook his head and put his head down. This sounds like something a car mechanic would do. So I never had it done.

I was concerned about my ankle and my rotator cuff more than anything at the time. It was hard to get around anyway with the bunions, the gout, the carpal tunnel, degenerative disc disease in my back, constant bleeding from my rectum and lower stomach pains, and my right kidney. I felt like someone was stabbing me with a knife. But I thought since they didn't have doctors to take care of the gastroenterology, nobody to give me a stress test, I would go ahead and take care of my ankle and rotator cuff first.

So we all decided to take the X-rays and send it off to Orthopedics. So November 8, 2017, they gave me an appointment with Dr. Jabczenski, the same doctor that evaluated me before with the toe splintering into my ankle. That was 2015 before I got flagged. He would not do anything at the time except cortisone shots. *Now* let me tell you what happened. When I got my appointment with him, his eyes were widened like he was in shock that I was back in his office. I mean, you have to think about this: you are a doctor, you didn't take care of your patient in the beginning, and he has been going through torment and pain for two years because you did not do your job properly. Now here he is again right in front of your face with more problems with the same ankle and the same toe that shattered to cause this torment.

To me, it looked like maybe he might be concerned. But if you read his notes and Dr. Lees's notes, you will see this doctor, if that is what you want to call him, was only really concerned about his motorcycle accident he said he had when I was in the office with him on my appointment date, but like I said, all of this can be obtained through my videotapes and recordings. I would love one of these doctors or these people to challenge me. Here is his report. It is very different from Dr. Lees:

Progress Notes

```
LOCAL TITLE: ORTHOPEDIC SURGERY CONSULT RESULT
STANDARD TITLE: ORTHOPEDIC SURGERY CONSULT
   DICT DATE: NOV 08, 2017@12:13      ENTRY DATE: NOV 09, 2017@08:38:18
   DICTATED BY: JABCZENSKI,FELIX F   EXP COSIGNER:
      URGENCY:                          STATUS: COMPLETED
```

PATIENT NAME: FRENCH,MICHAEL

HISTORY OF PRESENT ILLNESS: The patient was referred to me for
evaluation and treatment of his ankle. He has been having chronic
right ankle pain. It has been going on for several years. He has
had an MRI in the past. It showed some mild soft tissue swelling.
He has had a couple injections in the subtalar joint which have
helped. He denies specific history of injury. He is also
complaining of shoulder pain. He had an arthroscopy done several
years ago for impingement and that is hurting him more.

PHYSICAL EXAMINATION: On physical exam of the ankle, he does have
a definite soft tissue mass lateral to the ankle area. On full
range of motion of the ankle and the hindfoot, no bunions and no
forefoot abnormalities. On examination of the shoulder, he has got
limited range of motion secondary subacromial pain. He has good
strength to resistive internal and external rotation.

IMAGING: X-rays of the right ankle were normal. An MRI and CT
scan suggest a soft tissue mass laterally. This may be new from
the MRI that he did in the past. X-rays of the right shoulder were
reviewed and they were normal.

DIAGNOSIS:
1. Right ankle lateral soft tissue mass appears to be progressive.
2. Right shoulder possible rotator cuff tear.

PLAN: I discussed treatment options with him. The radiologist,
who did the CT, suggested an MRI of the ankle and so I ordered that
to give some further delineation of the soft tissue mass laterally.
I also will get an MRI of his right shoulder to rule out rotator
cuff. We will see him back in 6 weeks.

5409140/dm(11/08/2017 17:16:00)27043054

/es/ Felix F Jabczenski,MD
Orthopedic Surgeon
Signed: 11/09/2017 10:45

```
LOCAL TITLE: ORTHOPEDIC SURGERY CONSULT RESULT
STANDARD TITLE: ORTHOPEDIC SURGERY CONSULT
   DICT DATE: JUL 07, 2015@13:35      ENTRY DATE: JUL 08, 2015@10:17:03
```

PATIENT NAME
FRENCH,MICHAEL

CASA GRANDE, ARIZONA 85122

VISTA Electronic Medical Documentation
Printed at SOUTHERN ARIZONA VA HCS

Page 1

31

Wrongful Facts and Abuse

Well, I am very happy to see things are finally moving forward. I can't believe this is finally happening. My operations on my shoulder and ankle—Now maybe I can cut down on some of these pain pills and inflammatory drugs.

I know the inflammatory drugs are not good for my stomach and colon problems, and the pain pills are not good for anything to help your body, except for dulling the pain. But the problem is still there. So maybe now with the help of this doctor, two problems in my body will be gone. I am so happy. They sent me a letter already stating the pre-op appointment which is set for February 5, 2018, and my letter also has my surgery date for February 23, 2018.

My post-op appointment, which is after the surgery, is scheduled for March 8, 2018. These were two letters that were sent to me. I was upset with one of the letters and what it stated. In the letter, it has the date/time, the clinic, the location, telephone number, and the provider. When I read who the provider was, it was very disturbing to me. It said the provider's name was Harold Romero. So I called Dr.

Neustat's office. He would not speak to me. When I asked why, the receptionist, Randy, said, "He doesn't want to talk to you and he is not going to be your doctor anymore."

I asked, "Why is that?"

Randy stated in a very nasty and loud voice, "That is privileged information."

I knew in the back of my mind this was because of Susan MacDonald again. So I called the chief of staff's office. I had them page Larry Hoth and have him call me. Larry is part of the chief of staff. Larry admitted that it was because of Susan and that Harold Romero was just temporary. So really, I had no primary doctor, and if I got one, I would have to go through my whole history with him again in order for him to understand my problems and how severe they were. Attached below are the letters for pre-op, surgery, and post-op:

12/21/2017

MICHAEL FRENCH
CASA GRANDE AZ 85122

Dear Mr. Michael French,

Greetings from the Southern Arizona Health Care System…proudly serving Veterans since 1928. This is a reminder of the following clinic appointment:

****
****

LOCATION: BUILDING   50—2nd
FLOOR
Date/Time: MONDAY FEB 5, 2018
10:00 AM
Clinic: TUC SCL ORTHO JABCZEN
PRE OP
Location: BLDG 50, 2nd FLOOR
Telephone: (520) 629-4891
Provider: ROMERO, HAROLD

****
****

We suggest that you park in parking
lot G or F.

***NOTE: SERVICE ANIMALS ARE
NOT ALLOWED IN THE CLINIC/
PROCEDURE AREAS. PLEASE MAKE
ARRANGEMENTS TO HAVE YOUR
ANIMAL ATTENDED TO DURING
YOUR VISIT.***

Please arrive 15 minutes prior to you
scheduled appointment for check-in.

If you wish to reschedule or cancel this appointment, please call 1-800-471-8262 or 520-629-4891.

If you know you are not going to be able to keep this appointment, we would like to offer it to another veteran who is waiting so please call to reschedule or cancel at least 72 hours in advance.

We look forward to attending to your healthcare needs.

Reminder: 18 U.S.C 930 prohibits the possession of weapons on Federal property

Register online at www.myhealth.va.gov
Prescriptions are now available at www.myhealth.va.gov

This is a reminder of the following appointment:

Preliminary Appointment (PRE-OP) prior to actual surgery date.

PRE-OP Appointment: February 5, 2018

During this appointment, you will meet your Physician's Assistant (PA) and the orthopedic nurse, where you will do a History and Physical, sign consent forms and any other needed requirement for surgery. You will be sent to the lab to complete any needed blood work, EKG, and chest x-ray. Please be prepared for this appointment can take several hours.

Your surgery is scheduled for: February 23, 2018.

Your post-op appointment: March 8, 2018.

On January 24, 2018, I got a call from Orthopedics, and the nurse told me Dr. Jabczenski set an appointment to see me on January 31, 2018. I asked her, "What is it for?"

She said that he wanted to talk to me about my surgery. I told her thank you and I would be there on the thirty-first, which was a week from the twenty-fourth. Stephanie and I drove all the way to the Tucson VA. I proceeded to Orthopedics. After waiting for about an hour, I was called back to see Dr. Jabczenski. I was very upset by what he told me.

Stephanie had pushed me in a wheelchair. That was a lot better than using my cane. We used the wheelchair that was supplied by the hospital. He told me to stand up, and I did with Stephanie's help. He then said he wanted to see my ankle. I told him I would have to sit back down. So Stephanie helped me sit back down in the wheelchair. She also helped me out with my untied tennis shoe, sock, and pulled up my pant leg for him. He moved my foot around with his hand and squeezed on the ankle again. It hurt very bad. He grabbed my right arm by the forearm and tried to jerk it up. I said, "That hurts! What are you doing?"

He said he was just checking my motion. I told him he was not checking my motion because I was not lifting it. I told him, "You are lifting it and it hurts."

He then said, "I think you will be fine now."

I asked him, "What the heck do you mean?"

He then said, "I am not going to operate on you."

I said, "Is someone else going to?"

He then said I did not need an operation on the ankle or rotator cuff. I explained to him and reminded him that he said I needed it, and so did Dr. Lees and Dr. Neustat. Also Larry Hoth, the chief of staff because of the X-rays and MRIs and all of the imaging, not to mention my pain I was in now.

He laughed and said, "You will be fine. Just keep on taking your pain pills."

I could not believe what I was hearing. We left his office. Stephanie pushed me all the way to Larry Hoth's office. I am thankful Larry was there at the time. And on a recorded conversation, Larry said, "Oh no." He also said there had been a lot of complaints with Jabczenski. And he said, "You are not the only one." He told me a lot of vets had big problems after their surgeries with Jabczenski. This morning, before I had my appointment with Jabczenski, we had to go up on an elevator. There was another vet in a wheelchair. His leg was all bandaged from his ankle up to his hip. I asked him what the heck happened to him. He said Jabczenski had operated on him, and he was going to an appointment because he had infection all up his leg from his ankle to his hip from the surgery Jabczenski performed on him.

So I feel in my heart—after I thought about it and after him canceling me and listening to Larry Hoth, then talking to the vet—maybe he did not want to operate on me because maybe the director told him no more operations because of the vets he messed up. And most of all, I do believe God intercepted this because God knew what was going to happen to me.

If you think about things in a spiritual way and seek God, everything will unfold for you. Here are my notes below of what Jabczenski said and wrote down on January 31, 2018. *Also please read the first paragraph carefully. My right ankle was supposed to be operated on. In his notes, he states that he was going to operate on my left ankle. There is nothing wrong with my left ankle.* See what I mean by God intercepting?

Progress Notes

```
LOCAL TITLE: ORTHOPEDIC NOTE
STANDARD TITLE: ORTHOPEDIC SURGERY NOTE
   DICT DATE: JAN 31, 2018@19:44     ENTRY DATE: FEB 02, 2018@08:41:25
   DICTATED BY: JABCZENSKI,FELIX F    EXP COSIGNER:
      URGENCY:                        STATUS: COMPLETED
```

PATIENT NAME: FRENCH,MICHAEL

HISTORY OF PRESENT ILLNESS: The patient returns for followup. His
main problems are his right shoulder and his left ankle. His
shoulder hurts at night. He cannot sleep on that side. He has
some problems elevating it. With regard to the ankle, he has
always had some small cysts over the lateral ankle around the
fibula.

PHYSICAL EXAMINATION: With regard to the shoulder he actively
abducts to 50. I could passively get him up to about 170. He had
some tenderness over the biceps tendon. He had good strength to
resistive internal and external rotation. With regard to the
ankle, he had no cystic structures. Noted no swelling and no areas
of localized tenderness.

DIAGNOSTIC IMAGING: MRI of the shoulder was reviewed. It
demonstrates small periarticular thinning of the rotator cuff and a
small ganglion cyst in the posterior glenoid.

DIAGNOSIS:
1. Right shoulder biceps tendinitis.
2. Resolving small tissue swelling ankle.

RECOMMENDATION: With regard to the shoulder, I gave him a
cortisone shot using 40 mg of Depo-Medrol and 4 mL of 0.25%
Marcaine. Although he does have a ganglion cyst, it appears to be
not causing any neurological problems from the supraspinatus nerve.
With regard to the ankle, the small cysts that he had in the past
is resolved. He does have significant gout and he probably has
occasional swelling from the gouty arthropathy. I recommend he
stay with his gout medicines, pain pills, but there was no strong
indication for surgery on either the ankle or the shoulder. We
will see him back on an as-needed basis.

5977501/MF(02/01/2018 20:28:15)27991723

/es/ Felix F Jabczenski,MD
Orthopedic Surgeon
Signed: 02/05/2018 14:14

PATIENT NAME
FRENCH,MICHAEL

CASA GRANDE, ARIZONA 85122

VISTA Electronic Medical Documentation
Printed at SOUTHERN ARIZONA VA HCS

Page 1

32

They Are Trying to Force Me Out

I asked myself, "How can one person go through all of this incompetent rejection?" So far, let's add this up. They would not give me an endoscopy and colonoscopy. They made excuses about not having doctors. As far as my heart is concerned, when I thought I was set up for the stress test and EKG, they said they had no excuse that it was not set up, and I know for a fact it was. I was told never to call Mary Gilles's office ever again concerning my toxic water poisoning.

Neustat said to me that if I didn't get the blood in my bladder and cysts in my kidneys taken care of that I was playing with fire. I asked Neustat to set me up with a urologist and whoever I needed to see for these matters. He said he would, but nothing ever happened.

I was set up for operation on my right ankle and right rotator cuff. At the last minute, Dr. Jabczenski said he was not going to operate. And I'm glad because on his notes as you see here, he was going to operate on the left one, which was the wrong ankle. The right ankle is the one I had problems with. In my opinion, they never wanted to treat me at all from the beginning. That is why they drummed up that fake accusation from Susan MacDonald and flagged me.

But here I am again. So now, I guess they are trying to upset me enough just to give up. But I am not made that way. *I don't give up and never will!* In Nashville, at the VA, they were burning off my face the actinic keratosis. I have them still all over my face. I had to send to Nashville for my records Because they kept saying I did not have these cancers. It is kind of odd that this Tucson VA does not have the capability of connecting with another VA for your records. That is all a crock. But here I will include a progress note from Dr. King, a dermatologist, at the Tucson VA. His back was against the wall when he realized that I had copies of my records. Now here is what he had to say:

Progress Notes

```
Returned call at

If applicable: Patient could not be given an appointment with their assigned
Primary Care Provider due to following reason:
ED SAME DAY STATEMENT:

   PATIENT ADVISED HE/SHE CAN BE SEEN IN ED, BUT HE/SHE ELECTS TO:



   /es/ SUSAN MCKAY
   Medical Support Assistant
   Signed: 07/17/2014 13:40

   Receipt Acknowledged By:
   07/17/2014 16:33        /es/ MARIAN K. PAAS, RN
                                Staff RN

   07/18/2014 ADDENDUM                    STATUS: COMPLETED
   PT RETURNED YOUR CALL AND WOULD LIKE YOU TO CALL HIM BACK @

   /es/ SUSAN MCKAY
   Medical Support Assistant
   Signed: 07/18/2014 09:48

   Receipt Acknowledged By:
   07/18/2014 12:18        /es/ MARIAN K. PAAS, RN
                                Staff RN


   LOCAL TITLE: DERM NOTE
   STANDARD TITLE: DERMATOLOGY NOTE
   DATE OF NOTE: JUL 16, 2014@08:36    ENTRY DATE: JUL 16, 2014@08:36:57
       AUTHOR: KING,DANIEL C          EXP COSIGNER:
       URGENCY:           ,                 STATUS: COMPLETED

The patient returns to dermatology with a history of rosacea. This may be being
aggravated by niacin and lithium. He has minimal improvement with MetroGel. He
did scale and erythema around the nose and appeared area. He washes with Dove
Soap. He has a history of actinic keratosis treated in the past with
cryotherapy. He would like to be reexamined for potential future cancers.

Objective: Skin examination of the head, neck, chest, back, arms was conducted.
There is no active actinic keratosis noted at today's visit. There is scale in
the beard area along with erythema papules pustules and telangiectasia on the
face and forehead.
```

PATIENT NAME

FRENCH, MICHAEL

CASA GRANDE, ARIZONA 85122

VISTA Electronic Medical Documentation

Printed at SOUTHERN ARIZONA VA HCS

You can see now Dr. King, the dermatologist at the Tucson VA, has changed his tune. He had no other option. But you see that he says he can't see any of the cancers on me now, which is a lie. The cancers are on my face, arms, and neck. All he wants to do is give me some topical cream. When I was in Nashville, they were treating me very professionally and with the utmost care. Tucson don't want to spend a penny for the vets. Not one penny if they can get away with it. They think they might have gotten away with it with me. Well, that is enough for this chapter. Let's move along.

33

I Opened Up a Can of
Dirty Lying Worms

Well, after calling the pharmacy and finding out that Dr. Neustat was not my primary doctor anymore and some other doctor was signing off for my prescriptions, sometimes he did not even sign, so I did not get the prescriptions. I called Larry Hoth in the chief of staff's office, and he started giving me the run around too about everything—the operations that I was supposed to have, the pharmaceutical prescriptions, and so on. He told me that the new doctor was going to be cutting out my pain medication one pill at a time until I had no pain medication. I was supposed to get one hundred and eighty tablets of hydrocodone ten and three hundred twenty-five milligrams of acetaminophen. They were going to cut me down to one hundred and fifty, which would be five tablets a day instead of six. Then one hundred and twenty, which would be four tablets a day. Then ninety tablets a month, then sixty tablets a month, then thirty tablets a month, and then nothing.

I asked Larry, "Why?"

He said that the VA did not think I needed them.

I asked him, "Well, what about everything that is wrong with me? The bunions in my toes that were supposed to be operated on and were not, gout arthritis through my whole body, the carpal tunnel in my wrist, my ankle that was supposed to be operated on? My torn rotator cuff that doctor Jabczenski said to keep giving me pain meds for?"

Larry was acting like Dr. Jekyll and Mr. Hyde, and switching from a good personality to a bad personality. I could not believe the way Larry was talking to me. Larry told me one time, and it is on recording, that his wife had fibromyalgia, and she was on oxycodone for her pain. Larry told me that her doctor started to cut her down. But acting like a big shot, he went in when she went to the doctor for her visit. The doctor asked him because of the way he was talking, "Are you in the medical field?"

Larry told me that he said then to that doctor, "Yes" and showed him the credentials and talked the doctor into giving his wife more oxycodone. This is all on recording. He used his authority to influence other doctors. But in my case because of Susan MacDonald and the chief of staff's office, they hated me. And Larry said he could not do anything because he was scared to lose his job. So then I called the Ocotillo Clinic's AOD, which was Bob Klein, and spoke with him over the phone recorded conversation. I asked him, "How come Neustat does not want to be my doctor anymore?"

And he told me that it was because of his nurse/secretary, Susan MacDonald. I guess Susan was not happy with the pain she caused me for two years of not being able to be treated at the hospitals. And now since the flag is lifted, I still didn't get treated. I don't know what kind of relationship Dr. Stephen Neustat and Susan MacDonald have together, but it seems like to me, and I could only guess, that they are more than just a doctor and nurse the way this whole mess is playing out. Someone has got their nose stuck way up someone's butt. And I mean way up. So far up where they can't breathe right or think straight.

They told me that my new doctor would be Dr. Francisco Rivera. I told them I had not even met him and he was cutting my prescriptions down, not just the pain pills, but my potassium. Niacin he stopped completely and furosemide, which is a diuretic to keep the water off of my heart because I swell all of the time. I told Larry Hoth, "I don't want this doctor." I wanted Dr. Lees if I was going to be switched.

He told me that this Dr. Rivera was the head of all of the doctors and a great doctor. I told Larry, "I don't think he is a great doctor. Cutting out all of my medications and he has never even met me? That is not a great doctor in my opinion."

They set up a time for Rivera to call me at my home, and he never called. I reported this to Larry. He then said he would set up another time. Then Rivera failed to contact me on that call. So on March 30, 2018, Larry Hoth had given me a wrong number. This doctor was in Green Valley VA. So I found out the right number—520-399-2291— and contacted Dr. Rivera. He told me that he was going to keep cutting my medications unless I see him because he was going to be my primary doctor. And when I asked him how come Neustat wasn't going to be my doctor, he said it was a problem with Dr. Neustat's staff, meaning Susan MacDonald. So everything boils around Susan MacDonald, the little liar.

When I asked Dr. Rivera if he knew about my ankle, rotator cuff, toxic water problems, and so on, he said he didn't know anything about that and he would have to see me. I asked him, "Did you not look at my charts or my records to find out what is going on with my body?"

He said he did not know anything about it. He could not tell me one thing about my health problems and the reason why I have pains in different parts of my body. So how can a doctor want to give care for a patient when he doesn't know anything about him? How can he cut medication?

I was so fed up with this crap. Some of my meds still came with Dr. Neustat's name on it. How could that be if Dr. Neustat was not my doctor? I decided myself at this time this was not a place for me to go. It smelled like trouble was brewing somewhere. And what I mean by that is their evil trickery and schemes are not going to affect me this time. I am more on guard than I ever was in my life.

Trusting the Tucson VA is like driving your car one hundred miles an hour with duct tape over your eyes. You don't know when the crash is going to happen, but believe me, these people that call themselves doctors, the crash will happen. Even though I am in all of this pain and need operations, I am tired of pleading with these people for help. I will find another way. I do wish that our great president, Donald Trump, could know about all of these painful situations that they put vets through. So they have been doing this way before I bought my home in Arizona in February 2013. There are so many things they have done and it is in the newspaper, and I don't know why they keep getting away with it. Whenever I entered the doors of the Tucson VA, I felt really uneasy. I felt like evil was all around me. But anyway, I have got a clipping here from someone else that sadly went through this situation two years before I got here. So here it is:

Vet's Widow Wins $750,000 from VA

Ken Alltucker. *The Republic* | azcentral.com Published 9:20 p.m. MT April 20, 2015

A federal judge this month awarded $750,000 to the widow of a paraplegic man who died two days after arriving at the Tucson VA emergency room to seek treatment for stomach pain.

The judge found four doctors at the Southern Arizona VA Health Care System failed to meet standards of care for James Massara, whose complaints of stomach pain cascaded into dehydration and collapsed veins. The 56-year-old U.S. Navy veteran died less than 48 hours after arriving at the Tucson hospital.

U.S. Magistrate Judge Bernardo P. Velasco wrote in the April 6 judgment that "doctors in charge of Mr. Massara...fell below the appropriate standard of care" by failing to give him fluids and remove a bowel obstruction in time.

Massara's widow, Susan Massara, said that she was grateful for the award but misses her husband every day. The couple moved to Arizona in 2010 from Syracuse, N.Y.

"We missed out on so many things we planned to do here," said Susan, who also is paraplegic and relied on her husband for companionship and daily assistance. "I feel I was robbed of my spouse, my best friend and the love of my life."

Massara, who had been constipated for two days, was transported by ambulance to the Tucson hospital's emergency room on June 27, 2011, complaining of stomach pain, nausea and vomiting. Though his medical history, a physical exam and lab results suggested he was dehydrated, the VA's emergency-room doctor did not order fluids and there were no records of his fluid intake or output, court records show.

The judge also found fault with doctors' failure to manually remove a small-bowel obstruction or consult a surgeon.

Massara was admitted to the VA hospital the day after his ER visit and later to the hospital's intensive-care unit as his condition worsened. Doctors eventually tried to place a central line to administer fluids and draw blood from his collapsing veins for more tests, but Massara died just after 1 a.m. on June 29, 2011.

"The failure of the…physicians was the proximate cause of death of James Massara," Velasco wrote.

Susan Massara said she initially had no plans to sue the VA after her husband died, but she quickly grew frustrated when she tried to get answers about her husband's medical records.

"I was getting the runaround," Susan said, so she consulted a Tucson law firm. She sued and participated in a seven-day bench trial last November in U.S. District Court in Tucson.

In a statement, the VA offered condolences to the Massara family but noted the government has 60 days to appeal. The Department of Justice's Office of the Solicitor General will decide whether to appeal the case, the VA said.

Susan Massara has no plans to move from her small Tucson residence. She said she will buy a van with a ramp and room for her wheelchair so she can get around town more easily. She also plans to purchase a shower chair, which she says Medicare will not pay for.

"It's very bittersweet to think about my husband," Susan said. "I'd rather him be here."

I also spoke with Larry Hoth, and he explained to me of one of the recorded conversations that they wanted to give me versed and fentanyl for the operation. I asked Larry wasn't that fatal? Larry also said that I probably would not wake up ever. That was the chief of staff Larry Hoth. He also told me it was like a truth serum. But you see now. How scared these people have gotten me. They want me off their back so bad. To falsify statements to keep me away with a flag. To say if I come there I would be arrested and now when the flag is lifted they want to inject things inside of my body that can take my life from me. It wouldn't matter to them one bit especially after I signed a waiver for them to use the drugs they intend to use. This Tucson VA has the same reputation as the Phoenix VA. When they were exposed on the news with Judge Jeanine Pirro, and when Katherine Mitchell known as a whistleblower exposed them.

Both of these VAs are known for killing vets. But they are not going to kill me. Not in this book. Not in this lifetime. This is the God honest truth. I can produce my recordings. So now, I have to eagerly reach out to someone who cares.

34

Senator McCain Helps Vets? What a Joke. McCain to Blame

O n the date of August 2013, right after I moved to Arizona and bought my house in 2013, I went to the Tucson VA. I found out that the Phoenix VA was killing vets by not addressing their issues and they were dying. It was in the news on television with Judge Jeanine Pirro. Now that scared me, so I switched to Tucson. After repeatedly showing them documentation and pleading with them to help me with my toxic water poisoning from Camp Lejeune, they kept ignoring me. Even a urologist, Dr. Keldahl, grabbed Obama's papers that he had sent me—showing the TCE, PCE, vinyl chloride, benzene, and dry-cleaning fluid chemicals that I digested—and wadded them up and threw them on the floor and said, "I don't care!" I videotaped this incident. So after that and all the other refusals of addressing this problem, I went to Senator McCain's office.

I filed a complaint with my release of information papers and all of the paperwork he needed on August 27,

2013. I thought for sure he was working on this, and I felt in my heart something would be done about it. Month after month, I would call Senator McCain's office. Each month, they said they were working on this. They told me it takes a little time. Finally, I decided to start recording their conversations June 24, 2015. I spoke with Abigail at Senator McCain's Tucson office. She said to send a complaint form in.

I explained to her the complaint was the same. I needed a doctor to address the toxic water poisoning. The same thing happened on July 13, 2015, at Senator McCain's Tucson office. The same thing happened October 23, 2016, with Alisha at McCain's office in Tucson. I explained to Alisha that I haven't had treatment for almost a year and couldn't go to the VA because I was flagged with a falsified statement by Susan MacDonald in the Ocotillo Clinic. They said they were not aware of that. I told them they should be aware of it if they were working on my case.

The same thing happened October 24, 2016, with Susanne at Senator McCain's office in Tucson. Repeatedly, they said they were working on this, and I was having a lot of trouble getting treated at Tucson VA. They said they would take care of it. I needed Senator McCain to step in and straighten this problem out with the doctors and with this institution.

So I called back October 25, 2016, and spoke with Viviana. I called back October 26, 2016, and spoke with Ramone. They both told me that Senator McCain takes care of the vets and not to worry. So I waited with no treatment and then called back February 21, 2017, and spoke with Caleb. After I felt I was getting the runaround, I called back the same day February 21, 2017, and spoke with Ramone. Then August 29, 2017, I spoke with Wendy at Senator McCain's Phoenix office. She told me the form I filled out in 2013 had been canceled and the case was closed.

I was very upset. I didn't understand any reason why it should be closed. I had been calling them, tape recording every call. They kept telling me they were helping me. They kept saying McCain helped the vets. Why would my case be closed?

I decided to call Tucson again. On November 6, 2017, I spoke with Shay at McCain's office. She said the privacy act form was filled out but no letter was sent, so that is why the case was canceled. I explained to her that I did not send a letter. I filled out the letter that day in the office when the case was opened on August 27, 2013. She said she would check on it. So after all this time, all this aggravation, I found out that McCain's office was lying also and did not help the vets like he said.

But I then called Ramone in Senator McCain's Tucson office on February 23, 2018, and Ramone explained to me that Shay was in charge of my case and of everything that was going on and definitely working on it. I did not hear anything. No word, no mail, nothing from McCain's office. So after that date talking with Ramone, still I haven't heard anything back from McCain's office. And now still I am going through more grief from the Tucson VA.

Now in March of 2018, my medication was being cut. They were not doing anything for me. Tucson VA had not done anything for me except a couple of X-rays and MRIs and telling me *what was wrong with me! But they refused to do anything about it! And now they are wanting me to see a new doctor. His name is Rivera, and he is cutting my medication without even seeing me!*

I do not wish to have another doctor. I will not go to another doctor and start all over. I heard some bad things about this doctor and I never will see him. So this is what he wants to do. They will not reinstate me with Dr. Stephen Neustat because of Susan MacDonald. They will not let me prove or listen to my tape recordings to prove my innocence. Here are some of Dr. Rivera's notes. But before that, I have to explain that McCain's office is supposed to be working on all of this stuff for me. But in my heart, I don't think so. We will find out. Here are Rivera's notes now:

Progress Notes

/es/ FRANCISCO R RIVERA PABON
MD
Signed: 03/30/2018 16:32

03/30/2018 ADDENDUM   STATUS: COMPLETED
It is important to note that patient asked if he was going to receive the current
quantity of pain medication that he receives if he comes and see me to which I
told patient that tappering process would continue despite a face to face
appointment.

/es/ FRANCISCO R RIVERA PABON
MD
Signed: 03/30/2018 16:39

LOCAL TITLE: HISTORICAL NOTE
STANDARD TITLE: PRIMARY CARE ADMINISTRATIVE NOTE
DATE OF NOTE: MAR 23, 2018@12:51   ENTRY DATE: MAR 23, 2018@12:52:02
     AUTHOR: RIVERA PABON,FRANCI   EXP COSIGNER:
     URGENCY: STATUS: COMPLETED

Patient cancelled his appointment for 3/22/2018 stating that he did not know
about appointment.

Chart review reveals the following:

1. Chronic low back pain: Last MRI done in 6/15/2006 at another VA facility
revealed minor degenerative disc disease. Last images done at SAVAHCS of
lumbar
spine were done in 6/17/2013, revealing mild degenerative changes of lumbar
spine. Chart review reveals:

PATIENT NAME
FRENCH,MICHAEL

VISTA Electronic Medical Documentation
Printed at SOUTHERN ARIZONA VA HCS

Page 6

Progress Notes

5. Urine drug screening test dated 5/25/2017 was positive for ethyl glucuronide indicating EtOH intake in combination with chronic opioid therapy.

Given the above, I recommended for patient to be tappered off opioid therapy (see Addendum to Medication Controlled RX Inquiry dated 3/6/2018). I will follow taper plan recommended by Pain Pharmacist (see Addendum to E-Consult Pain Management Consult dated 3/7/2018).

I don't drink alcohol. And that report from my lab and urine work that he is talking about, if you notice the date on it, it is one year before this date of his notes with this thing they call a doctor. At that time in my life one year ago, I had flu-like symptoms and was sick. I had a runny nose and it was stuffed up so, in fact, I took from Walmart the Equate cold and flu pain reliever, fever-reducer, and cough suppressant. This medication is related to Nyquil, but it is a cheaper version called Equate. I found out that it contains 10 percent alcohol. I was taking this during the time period of the testing, and that is all.

Now why is this doctor going back a year? Nobody else said anything about this (I know why)! These people—the whole staff and everybody in this institution—want me out. This is why all of this is going on. They went back a year to try to find something or get something on me a whole year. Why didn't they do it then? And my testing now has nothing. And there's nothing past that date when I was sick.

These people have to be exposed. I have all of the tape recordings and videotapes about these people. I don't intend to see this doctor. I refuse to let this hospital hurt me or lie about me again. I will not go there anymore. I have recorded lies from every one of them that ever spoke to me. Honorably dishonored again.

Now, since Senator McCain's office is supposed to be working on this stuff for me, I will give them a call. On April 19, 2018, I called Senator McCain's office in Tucson. I spoke with Selena and Susanne. So I spoke with them for about a half an hour, asking them about my case. First,

Selena answered the phone and acted like a junior high person by stuttering and not knowing anything. Finally, she said, "Wait a second, I will get someone to help you."

Susanne introduced herself, and after about ten or fifteen minutes from her, I finally got a straight answer. With an angry voice, because I was very persistent, she told me the date it was open and the date it was closed a year later. I explained to her that Shay was supposed to be working on the case. She said, "Absolutely not." The case was expired, and that I had to renew it every year. Nobody ever told me this. Nobody ever mentioned this at all from McCain's office. McCain's staff has lied to me continuously.

When I opened my case in 2013, Susanne said it expired in 2014. I have been dragged along and lied to all of the time. Here is my opinion of McCain and his office. As far as Senator McCain is concerned in my mind, body, and soul, he is as fake as a rubber check. God does not let people walk the face of this earth in achieving anything in any way by saying they are taking care of vets or other people and lying about it, especially empowered people like McCain. He was only concerned about himself and the power he had or he thought he had. I'm gut sick of hearing about him being a prisoner of war, and one of the reasons why is because in one of the pictures taken in the prisoner of war camp, he was smiling. In my opinion, I wouldn't be smiling unless I made some type of a deal with the people who had me imprisoned. Does that make sense? Or does that make sense? So once again, honorably dishonored.

35

Senator Flake Is a Fake

Well, I am tired, worn-out, disgusted, and hurt all over my body. And I am scared of what might happen to me with all of these internal problems. Stephanie and I want very much to get married. The doctor's notes also said I am a fertility risk. I don't know exactly what that means. But I do want to have one child if not more before I die. I want to have a house paid for in Chicago where Stephanie and the children do not have to worry. When I die, Stephanie will get my disability from the Marine Corps, also my social security. That will help her through life and help her take care of our children.

I called the Hines VA in Chicago, and some people that I had met before still worked there. They welcomed me with open arms. They wished me the best of luck in finding a new home in Chicago and selling mine in Arizona. Stephanie and I put a lot of work into this house that we have now. The real estate agents and investors are trying to buy it for a low price just to flip it. There is no way that I am going to give this home away to them for their prices.

Like I said, Stephanie and I have blood, sweat, and tears in this house from the work we put into it. We put in all new appliances with five-year warranties, a brand-new air conditioner with ten-year warranty, new hot water heater with six years of warranty, and the list goes on. From top to bottom, the sinks, faucets, marble vanities, pool pumps, fountain pumps, new koi pond, eight-foot-high and fourteen-foot waterfall on saltwater pool—you ask me why do I want to leave all of this? And I will tell you, this is not home to Stephanie and me. We are both from the Midwest. We miss the four seasons and flat out, plainly, I cannot figure out how to decorate a cactus for Christmas! I will tell you the truth. It is a very *sticky situation*. Try it sometime, you will see what I mean.

Well, the wheels are in motion with the real estate people, here and in Chicago. I just hope my health is up to moving all of this stuff. Stephanie and I personally moved everything out here. But right now, with all this pain, I don't know how I am going to get through it. I have one other thing that Stephanie and I did to try to seek some help. We went to Senator Flake's office in Tucson, Arizona. But before we went there, I called his office at 520-575-8633 and spoke with a man by the name of Jeremy Thompson.

This was on April 4, 2018. My appointment was supposed to be April 5, 2018, but I was not feeling good, so I asked him over the phone if I could reschedule, and he was very polite and set a date for April 11, 2018. Stephanie was preparing all of my notes and recordings and the progress notes that I had obtained from Release of Information before the Tucson VA realized it because they like to go into people's files like mine and reword things to try to cover their tracks. But in most cases, at least 99.5 percent of the time, I recovered what was said by doctors, staff, and others before they could change the wording in my files.

When I confronted them about this, they just froze like they were zombies, mouths open and nothing to say. It really freaked them out, not to mention the videotapes and tape recordings. Stephanie and I were both wired at all times, even at Senator Flake the Fake's office. So now it is time to meet Jeremy Thompson, the representative for Senator Flake the Fake. We arrived in the corridor at his office on Wednesday April 11, 2018, at 8:55 a.m. Prior to this date, Jeremy Thompson had sent me a letter to my home for Release of Information. I did not fill it out. I brought it with me to the meeting. If I did sign and fill this release of information out, he was just going to get all lies.

So Stephanie prepared all notes of the doctors and staff and whoever and videotapes and tape recordings. We figured that we would arm ourselves with the truthful ammunition. *Oh no! Did I say armed and ammunition? I hope Susan Macdonald doesn't hear this. She will say I am coming with guns and to kill everybody again! Ha ha ha!* Okay, with all of the joking aside, we are prepared with our evidence to show Jeremy. Get ready for the representative of Flake the Fake.

Jeremy came out and invited us into his office and was very polite. Stephanie and I introduced ourselves, and so did Jeremy. We shook hands, Jeremy offered us some water, and we said we just finished some. Then I started explaining to him from the beginning. I showed him articles and statements from Camp Lejeune toxic water contamination. This is what I showed him, and I explained to him that I have several of these health issues that have been diagnosed. Some of them I have been treated for at the Nashville VA and Hines VA in Chicago. But the Tucson VA will not address these issues, even though my primary doctor Stephen Neustat diagnosed some more problems that I didn't know about that were concerning the toxic water contamination. He had diagnosed hepatic steatosis, renal toxicity, I had blood in my bladder, and on the list, it said bladder cancer, but the Tucson VA will not go any further addressing these issues. Nashville VA took out cancerous polyps out of my throat, and on the list, it says esophageal cancer. Anyway, below is the report and list from President Obama. This is what I presented to Jeremy.

IB 10-449
December 2013

Camp Lejeune Water Contamination (Historical)

Description

From at least the 1950s to the 1980s, Veterans and family members living or serving at the U.S. Marine Corps Base Camp Lejeune in North Carolina were potentially exposed to drinking water contaminated with chemicals known as volatile organic compounds (VOCs), including industrial solvents and components of fuels.

On August 6, 2012, President Obama signed into law the "Honoring America's Veterans and Caring for Camp Lejeune Families Act of 2012." For Veterans who served at Camp Lejeune between 1957 and 1987, this law provides VA health care for 15 medical conditions. Support for health care costs may also be provided for family members for these conditions once new regulations are published.

Illnesses or Conditions

The new law requires VA to provide health care for the following illnesses or conditions:

- Bladder cancer
- Breast cancer
- Esophageal cancer
- Female infertility
- Hepatic steatosis
- Kidney cancer
- Leukemia
- Lung Cancer
- Miscarriage
- Multiple myeloma
- Myelodysplastic syndromes
- Neurobehavioral effects
- Non-Hodgkin's lymphoma
- Renal toxicity
- Scleroderma

Veterans

To be eligible for care under this law, the Veteran must have served on active duty at Camp Lejeune for not fewer than 30 days between January 1, 1957, and December 31, 1987.

Veterans who are eligible for care under the Camp Lejeune authority, regardless of current enrollment status with VA, will not be charged a copayment for health care related to the above illnesses or conditions, nor will a third party insurance company be billed for these services. Copayments for care unrelated to the above illnesses or conditions may be applicable.

IB 10-449

Page 1 of 2

36

Jeremy's Response

Jeremy began looking over some of my notes and evidence. I came to the part about calling Dr. Neustat, and Susan MacDonald would not let me talk to him. I explained to him how I reported Susan MacDonald to the chief of staff's office and Stan Holmes, who was the chief of Primary Care. I reported Susan two times. Everybody in the hospital shut their doors on me, or you might say turned their backs on me. They did not want to spend any money on me. Not only me, but other vets also. I could not be concerned too much about the other vets. I had feelings for them, but I was in pain and very concerned about my life. He kept looking over documents, and he listened to a piece of the recording, but when it started to play, he said he did not care to listen to any of it. Stephanie and I were sure and very hopeful and believed through what Jeremy said on the phone that Senator Flake would help us. So we had spun off CDs and videotapes from our computer that we had downloaded for Senator Flake. We were going to leave all of the notes, CDs, and videos with Jeremy.

He said to us that he did not want them. I said, "But you have to have them. This is the evidence!"

He again said, as he was picking up the notes that I had spread out on his desk, "I do not want them."

I was very disgusted at this point. Why didn't he want them? The notes were rock-solid proof; the recordings were rock-solid proof; the videos were rock-solid proof. If you take my evidence, all of your work is done. He told me that the only thing he wanted me to do was sign a release of information that he would gather my reports from the VA. I told him that the only thing he was going to get were lies. They were not going to tell the truth about what they did and what they did not do for me. I asked him if I could call Senator Flakes office in Phoenix Arizona, and then I asked him if Senator Flake would be there.

I told him I wanted to speak with Senator Flake either on the phone or in person. He told me, "Senator Flake does not do that."

I told him, "I have the right to speak with him. How can I contact him?"

He told me, "I cannot help you with that."

I also explained to him about Dr. Harsha, a dentist at the Tucson VA that I was seeing, and Dr. Cornelius, who is the Chief dentist over all of the dentists. He wanted to know in-depth what happened. They all know that I had headaches. They listed them as migraines, my primary doctor, Dr. Neustat. But Dr. Harsha, my dentist, took X-rays of my mouth and said to me that I had one of my implants in my sinuses, my right implant. Dr. Harsha then sent me to two outside specialists, meaning not connected with the VA. Dr. Harsha made sure that the VA paid for these appointments.

First, I saw Dr. Lew, a maxillofacial surgeon. He was really nice but very concerned about me. He had X-rayed me and showed me where the right implant was in my sinuses. He told me I needed to have treatment and/or have it removed and replaced correctly. He explained to me that the VA would have to set up the appointments for me to see him again. He said he would contact Dr. Harsha at the VA dentistry. Dr. Harsha did not say anything to me about Dr. Lew, but he did set up another appointment with another dentist in which his title was periodontics and implantology. His name was Dr. E. Daniel Gall, a D.D.S. in Tucson, Arizona.

He did the same thing as Dr. Lew. He took X-rays and pictures of my mouth. He also said that I had the implant in my sinuses. He told me that would cause problems in my life and needed to be addressed. There needed to be a type of procedure done. He said he would contact Dr. Harsha.

Well, weeks went by, and then months went by. I explained to Jeremy that nothing was happening and that I had called Dr. Harsha, and he said that the specialists had not contacted him. So I called the specialists. Now I did not get a written report from Dr. Lew about what he needed to do for me, but I did get and do have a message on my phone that Dr. Lew had left stating that I needed to start some type of treatment as soon as possible and that he had, in fact, contacted Dr. Harsha and left messages. I also called Dr. Gall's office. They said the same thing. They said they had sent a letter to Dr. Harsha.

I asked them to send me a letter. Here is what the letter says, and here are two of my X-rays from Dr. Lew.

Clyde M. Robinson, D.D.S., M.Sc.D.
E. Daniel Gall, D.D.S.
Periodontics / Oral Implantology
2330 North Rosemont
Tucson, Arizona 85712
(520)327-0263

Mr. French:

This letter is to inform you that we have not received any updates from Dr. Harsha regarding your status. Dr. Gall sent him an e-mail back in March '15 and a Therapy Progress report and we have not heard from him since he referred you to us. Dr. Mackelprang is our new associate and he is happy to see you for an exam and go from there to determine what needs to be done. As of now we cannot do anything till Dr. Mackelprang sees you and comes up with a treatment plan. If you need any further assistance or questions, please feel free to contact the office.

Thank you.
Leticia

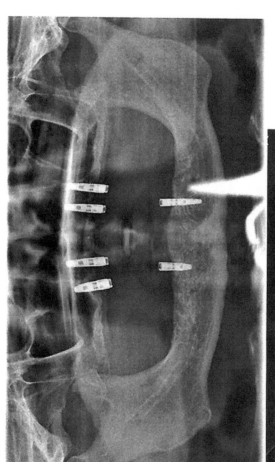

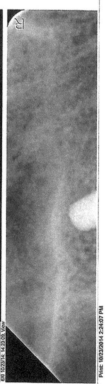

French, Michael

TLew
Associates in Oral and
Maxillofacial Surgery

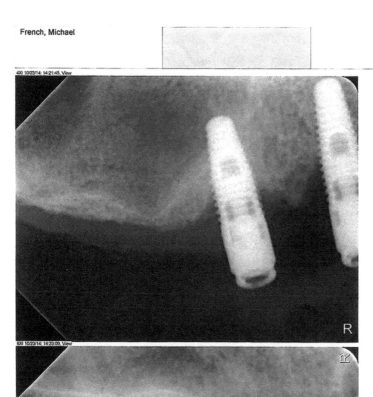

I reached out to Dr. Harsha again, and asked him, "Are you sure the two doctors, Dr. Lew and Dr. Gall, did not leave you any messages about how they wanted to treat me?"

He answered no.

Anyway, back to Jeremy at Senator Flake's office. Jeremy started talking to me about a lawsuit against the government. He said I could get a pretty good dollar amount if I got the right lawyer. I told him I wasn't worried about lawsuits. I was worried about and wanted to have reckoning of all of the stuff I had been through. Jeremy then said to sign a consent form so he could get release of information and speak with them and ask them questions at the Tucson VA. I told him again, "I have all of my records here, the real ones. The ones I got as soon as I was finished with my appointments with the doctors. Stephanie and I went to Release of Information and got the records as soon as possible. When they realized about investigations because of me, they revised the records. They were not the same as the original records, but I have them here in your office and videotapes and tape recordings."

Jeremy stated that he did not want any of them. I am sure Senator Flake instructed his workers, his staff, what to do and what not to do. That is how politicians are. They do not care about the little guys, and they will not rock the boat. It jeopardizes their political position. And Jeremy did not want the truth either. It would jeopardize his job with Flake.

I proved to Jeremy that day, right in front of his face, how everything that I said was the truth. As far as Harsha and 99 percent of the Tucson VA and staff is concerned, there is a small 1 percent that I respect who have honored me. I will create a list off the top of my head to put as acknowledgments in my book. I want them to know that they are honored also. You can see by the reports of Dr. Harsha, first he is saying that I got infected and I have the implant in my sinuses. He gave me Tylenol 3 for the pain. I still have his prescription bottles that he gave me. Then he got mad at me after he had already given them to me, and I picked them up from the pharmacy. It is not that I needed them. It is because I was already getting hydrocodone for my other pains.

I guess that makes sense in a way but also it shows that he knew and saw my infection from the implant. He lied about everything. He told me he did not hear from the specialists that he sent me to. Dr. Harsha also sent me to Dr. Tamara L. Tom, a dentist in the Tucson VA. She started to examine me. My gum was swollen with yellow pus. I told her not to touch it. She had a needlelike object probing the gum line of each implant. It hurt in the implants that were not infected, and I told her, do not touch the infected one. But she tried to anyway, and it hurt like heck.

I pushed her hands away and jumped up. She called me a baby. I don't know if she was Japanese or what. The only thing that went through my mind, if she was Japanese and that she had a vendetta against Americans and was trying to get even by hurting me because we kicked Japan's butt after they bombed Pearl Harbor. I don't know, but that is how I felt.

I reported her to the Patient Advocate's office, Vicky McManaman. I had to keep calling because nothing had been done. Finally, she proceeded with my complaint. But this also proves that I had pus and also an infected implant. Now Harsha said I didn't. He sent me out to the specialist, hoping that they would find nothing wrong with me. But it backfired on him and also on the chief dentist, Dr. Cornelius. Now put it all together, for a man with wisdom can understand what I am about to say. Cornelius was also having meetings in the morning with the chief of staff. So it is self-explanatory. They all got together in their little conspiracy to keep me out of the VA. They did not want to spend any money. Below, I have proof.

First of all, Harsha says I did have the implant in my sinus and infection. That is why he sent me to a specialist, *he says*. Here are Dr. Harsha's notes below:

Progress Notes

```
   LOCAL TITLE: DENTAL NOTE
STANDARD TITLE: DENTISTRY E & M NOTE
DATE OF NOTE: OCT 14, 2014@08:35    ENTRY DATE: OCT 14, 2014@08:38:50
    AUTHOR: HARSHA,BRUCE B      EXP COSIGNER:
    URGENCY:                        STATUS: COMPLETED

Patient Name: FRENCH,MICHAEL
  Visit: S: Oct 14, 2014@08:00 TUC DENTAL HARSHA.
  Primary PCE Diagnosis: 525.10 (UNSP ACQUIRED ABSENCE TEETH).
  Dental Category: 15-CLASS IV.  Treatment Status: Maintenance.

Completed Care:
  (D5510) DENTUR REPR BROKEN COMPL BAS.  DX: (525.10).

Dental Alerts:
  Allergic to PCN
  SINGLE IMPLANTS 4,6,10,12,22,27

- - - - - - - - - - - - - - - - - - - - - - - - - - - - - - -
Pt identity verified x 2
Pt consents to today's treatment
Pt has hole in lower denture baseplate which was repaired at time of exam.
Pt has experienced periodic pain around upper right implants.  Pt was
informed at the time of placement that one is in the sinus.  CT confirms
this.
Plan:  Will refer to fee basis oral surgeon to see if anything
should/could be done.
Disposition: refer to Associates in Oral and Maxillofacial Surgery  (will
attempt to copy CT go disc.)

/es/ BRUCE B. HARSHA
DDS
Signed: 10/14/2014 08:38
```

VISTA Electronic Medical Documentation

Printed at SOUTHERN ARIZONA VA HCS

Page 1

Progress Notes

```
LOCAL TITLE: DENTAL NOTE
STANDARD TITLE: DENTISTRY E & M NOTE
DATE OF NOTE: NOV 03, 2014@14:31     ENTRY DATE: NOV 03, 2014@14:31:36
      AUTHOR: HARSHA,BRUCE B     EXP COSIGNER:
      URGENCY:                        STATUS: COMPLETED
```

        *** DENTAL NOTE Has ADDENDA ***

The patient called asking for me and told the dental receptionist that it was an
emergency. When I answered the phone he stated that he was waiting to be
appointed for a new CT scan and had not heard from anyone. I was unaware that
he was to get a new one and stated the same. He says that Dr. Lew (fee basis
oral surgeon) wanted one. I told him I would have to call Dr. Lew and find out
what he wanted. I called Dr. Lew's office and had to leave a message. I will
call Mr. French back as soon as I learn what Dr. Lew wants.

/es/ BRUCE B. HARSHA
DDS
Signed: 11/03/2014 14:34

11/06/2014 ADDENDUM   STATUS: COMPLETED
I talked with Dr. Lew who has reviewed the patient' last CT scan. He does not
have an definitive recommendation for patient's dental complaints. He says that
even though the implant is in the sinus, there is no evidence of pathology
around it. He will discuss with his colleagues and let me know if there is a
recommendation. I called patient and informed him of this. Evidently the
patient is to see a neurologist about his eye pain which might shed some light
on this.

/es/ BRUCE B. HARSHA
DDS
Signed: 11/06/2014 11:05

11/06/2014 ADDENDUM   STATUS: COMPLETED
Dr. Lew called me and told me that he felt there was no treatment indicated at
this time and that he informed patient of that. I will plan no further tretment
until recare.

/es/ BRUCE B. HARSHA

PATIENT NAME   ) | **VISTA Electronic Medical Documentation**

FRENCH,MICHAEL

                                        Printed at SOUTHERN ARIZONA VA HCS

·Progress Notes

```
LOCAL TITLE: DENTAL NOTE
STANDARD TITLE: DENTISTRY E & M NOTE
DATE OF NOTE: FEB 17, 2015@09:15     ENTRY DATE: FEB 17, 2015@09:21:14
        AUTHOR: HARSHA,BRUCE B        EXP COSIGNER:
        URGENCY:                          STATUS: COMPLETED

Patient Name: FRENCH,MICHAEL
  Visit:  S: Feb 17, 2015@09:00 TUC DENTAL HARSHA.
  Primary PCE Diagnosis: 525.9 (DENTAL DISORDER NOS).
  Dental Category: 15-OPC, Class IV.    Treatment Status: Maintenance.

Completed Care:
  (D9999) ADJUNCTIVE PROCEDURE.  DX: (525.9).

Dental Alerts:
  Allergic to PCN
  SINGLE IMPLANTS 4,6,10,12,22,27

- - - - - - - - - - - - - - - - - - - - - - - - - - - - - -
Pt identity verified X2.
Pt here to discuss options regarding implant #4.
Pt has already been referred to fee basis oral surgeon who felt that
surgical intervention was not indicated at this time.
Pt states that he continues to have infections and drainage.
Plan: will refer to fee basis periodontist, Dr. Dan Gall who has
experience with dental implants.
Disposition:
Arrangements made with his office to be seen March 2.

/es/ BRUCE B. HARSHA
DDS
Signed: 02/17/2015 09:21

Receipt Acknowledged By:
02/17/2015 14:56        /es/ Michael E. Bays, D.O.
                             Physician - Ear, Nose and Throat
```

PATIENT NAME.....

FRENCH,MICHAEL

VISTA Electronic Medical Documentation

Printed at SOUTHERN ARIZONA VA HCS

Page 8

Progress Notes

06/16/2015 12:35   /es/ BRUCE B. HARSHA
                             DDS

06/16/2015 ADDENDUM   STATUS: COMPLETED
The patient called me and informed me that he has an "infected implant" again
and wants renewal of his antibiotic and peridex prescriptions. None of my
observations of him have ever demonstrated an active infection intraorally
around his implants   (erythema,swelling, purulence or other drainage, mobility
of the implant). Nor have either the periodontist nor oral surgeon who we
referred him to (whether there is some occult problem in his sinus I cannot
speculate on). I don't have a problem renewing his peridex but I cannot renew
his antibiotic without seeing him to be sure that there is in an oral infection
within my scope of practice. I offered to see the patient tomorrow and he
declined. I have informed my schedulers that he will need to come in and I am
happy to overbook him. I will renew his peridex when he tells me how he wants
it delivered.

/es/ BRUCE B. HARSHA
     DDS

PATIENT NAME   VISTA Electronic Medical Documentation
FRENCH,MICHAEL   Printed at SOUTHERN ARIZONA VA HCS

Progress Notes

```
LOCAL TITLE: DENTAL NOTE
STANDARD TITLE: DENTISTRY E & M NOTE
DATE OF NOTE: JUL 15, 2015@15:50     ENTRY DATE: JUL 15, 2015@15:50:16
    AUTHOR: HARSHA,BRUCE B        EXP COSIGNER:
    URGENCY:                          STATUS: COMPLETED

    *** DENTAL NOTE Has ADDENDA ***
```

Pt called and demanded that I call him today. I called patient and patient was very ademant that I do something to get rid of his pain. He questioned why I referred him to an oral surgeon and a periodontist and I said that I sent him because I was trying to help him. He kept repeating questions about why "they" (meaning the VA in Tennessee) put an implant in his sinus. I told him they did not do it on purpose and that it indeed does happen from time to time ususally without consequences. Pt insists that I do something and wants to know why I won't. I told him I can't do anything because I do not know what to do or how to help him. I informed him that if he is unhappy he should talk to Dr. Cornelius, the dental chief, because I can think of no way I can make him happy.

```
/es/ BRUCE B. HARSHA
DDS
Signed: 07/15/2015 15:55


Receipt Acknowledged By:
07/16/2015 09:32       /es/ CURTIS A CORNELIUS
                       Chief Dental


07/16/2015 ADDENDUM                STATUS: COMPLETED
Veteran will be placed in my patient load, I will become his PDP.

/es/ CURTIS A CORNELIUS
Chief Dental
Signed: 07/16/2015 09:33
```

VISTA Electronic Medical Documentation
Printed at SOUTHERN ARIZONA VA HCS

So now after viewing Dr. Harsha's notes and lies about Dr. Lew and all of his wishy-washy statements, you will see that this doctor—if that is what you want to call him because I don't—has no credibility.

So now we are moving on to Dr. Tamara Tom. You will see in her notes that it verifies my infection in my implant. Well, here it is:

Progress Notes

```
LOCAL TITLE: DENTAL NOTE
STANDARD TITLE: DENTISTRY E & M NOTE
DATE OF NOTE: SEP 16, 2014@11:10     ENTRY DATE: SEP 16, 2014@11:17:36
     AUTHOR: TOM,TAMARA L        EXP COSIGNER:
     URGENCY:                        STATUS: COMPLETED
```

Patient Name: FRENCH,MICHAEL
  Visit: S: Sep 16, 2014@10:30 TUC DENTAL TOM U/C.
  Primary PCE Diagnosis: V72.2 (DENTAL EXAMINATION).
  Dental Category: 15-CLASS IV. Treatment Status: Maintenance.

Completed Care:
  (D0220) INTRAORAL PERIAPICAL FIRST. Tooth: 4. DX: (V72.2).
  (D0230) INTRAORAL PERIAPICAL EA ADD. Tooth: 6. DX: (V72.2).
  (D0140) LIMIT ORAL EVAL PROBLM FOCUS. DX: (V72.2).

Presentation/Chief Complaint:
  Patient presents for limited oral evaluation
  I have a lot of pain in the upper right side. Reports that the
  maxillary right implants have a dental infection which resulted in
  expression of pus.
History of Present Illness (HPI):
  Patient states that a few days ago he placed pressure on the upper
  right implants and expressed a yellow/white purulent drainage.

Progress Notes

Oral Examination:
  Other:
    #4 and #6 buccal vestibule slightly tender to
    palpation, upon palpation there is no expression
    of purulence. Implants in position #4 and #6 are
    nonmobile with #6 having a perio pocket of approx
    7mm on the lingual

Assessment/Plan:
  Possible #4 and #6 chronic peri-implantitis.
  Reviewed CT scan (completed 8/28/2014) which shows that the implant
  in position #4 may have perforated the sinus. Will evaluate at next
  visit with Dr. Harsha. Patient repeatedly demanded antibiotics.
  After review of chart it was noted that Dr. Bays (ENT) had Rx'd

PATIENT NAME.

FRENCH, MICHAEL

VISTA Electronic Medical Documentation

Printed at SOUTHERN ARIZONA VA HCS

Page 2

276

Progress Notes

Clindamycin 300mg for dental infection written on 9/15/2014. Patient
appears to have no recollection of this medication.
Upon perio probing of gingival around tooth, patient states that it was very
painful and pushed hands of dentist out of mouth. Patient states that he wanted
to leave and demanded antibiotics.

/es/ TAMARA L TOM
DENTIST
Signed: 09/16/2014 15:31

PATIENT NAME

FRENCH, MICHAEL

VISTA Electronic Medical Documentation

Printed at SOUTHERN ARIZONA VA HCS

Now, if you can read Dr. Tamara Tom's notes correctly, you can see that I had infection. Also, you can see where I told her not to stick the probe into my gums, but she did anyway. So she was truthful for saying that I pushed her hands away and jumped out of the chair.

Next is the complaint. Here we have our forgetful Patient Advocate, Vicky McManaman Med., CHR Senior Patient Advocate. *Wow!* A senior patient advocate. This is a pretty impressive title. Like I said, this took at least fifteen phone calls before I could finally get in contact with her to see what she was doing about my complaint. My complaint was filled out September 16, 2014, and she said the investigation took a *whole three days. Wow!* And that date was September 19, 2014. The notes are self-explanatory below. First, her letter to me about her being tardy. *Ha! Ha!*

DEPARTMENT OF
VETERANS AFFAIRS
Southern Arizona VA
Health Care System
Tucson, AZ 85723

10/23/14

Dear Mr. French:

This letter is in regards to your request for a copy of the contact note you called to remind me about getting you had signed the request form. I did print the note out and saw your release form did not have your address, I laid it aside and forget to look up your mailing address to mail it out I regret my tardiness for failing to mail it sooner. SAVAHCS strives to provide quality and compassionate care to all of our Veteran patients. On behalf of a grateful nation thank you for your service to our country. If you have any further questions please contact me at the Patient Advocate Office, 520-629-4933.

Sincerely,

Vicky McManaman, Med., CHR
Senior Patient Advocate

So now, here is Senior Vicky McManaman Med. CHR, Senior Patient Advocate. She must be really proud of herself. Oh, by the way, I spoke with her about other things that the doctors in the hospital wasn't doing for me. And I had them on my recorder, and Stephanie and I brought it to her office. When we told her that we had recordings and videotapes of everything, she freaked out, and said it was against the law to do that. I said, "Why do you have video cameras up and down each hall?"

As she was stuttering, I pulled out the Arizona federal and state laws on recording or videotaping called the one-party consent law. This means that if you are recording, it is perfectly legal in the state of Arizona. Here are the statutes for the state first: A.R.S. & 13-3005-3012(9). Federal Statute for Arizona is 18 U.S.C. 2511 (2)(d).

After I explained this to Vicky McManaman, the Senior Patient Advocate, she did not even want to see the statutes. She did not want to listen to any of the recordings at all. I found out later on that she has morning meetings with the chief of staff and the whole gang. She doesn't care for the patients likes and advocates as she is supposed to. *They are all up each other's butts* in their little meetings. *They don't care about the patients. They only care about the money that is spent, meaning they don't want to spend any money.*

Now here is Vicky's investigation that took a whole three days, and I didn't hear anything for over a month later when I had to keep calling about fifteen times. So here it is:

Cover Sheet	
ROC Number:	678.201401805
Date of Contact:	09/16/2014
Information Taken By:	MCMANAMAN, VICKY
Contact Phone/Fax:	NONE
Contacting Entities:	Patient / Methods of Contact: Visit
Congressional Contact:	NONE

Patient	
Patient:	FRENCH, MICHAEL / Treatment Status: Outpatient

Issue	
Issue Description:	Today pt presented with a concern after he was seen in the dental clinic with an appt and provider was Dr. Tom. His gums were swollen , irritated and pus was excreting when touched, he had placed a touch on the upper right area causing the draining, Dr Bays prescribed an anti-biotic 9/15 (according to the note to tx both his dx on the sore throat and nasal area, which could also be to be to help with the upper right implant problem). 1) the dentist hurt with pressing on the gums and continued to do so after asking it to be stopped 2) had asked for numbing if continued to touch inside the area that was infected 3) feels that the delivery of care was rough and poking created more pain Pt wanted to be seen by his regular dentist Dr Harsha for follow up and would let me know when the best date and time would be so he could arrange with another VA appt, already had a appt for 10/14 if none available would keep that appt. I explained that when a supervisor has been asked to address the complaint with the employee I can only be advised that a meeting or talk did take place and I am not priveledged as personnel records are confidential.

Resolution			
ROC Issue Details:			
Issue Code	Location	Facility Service or Section	Employee Involved
SC01	Dental Clinic	DENTAL	ESQUIBEL, GREGORY L DDS

Resolution Text:	Agreed that I would address with the Chief, Dental Service on the pt's concern about his visit with the dentist and arrange for him to see his regular Dentist Dr Harsha sooner after he agreed to call me on when a good day would be for the appt. I contacted Dr Esquibel and discussed the pt's dissatifaction on the care he received and wnting to see Dr Harsha, and if no sooner appt available with Dr Harsha than the 10/14/14 appt he would keep that appt. On 9/17 I was advised Dr Harsha has clinics on certain days (Monday, Tuesday or Thursday) but would have the Admin Officer check for an available clinic appt if one was open on the pt's next appt elsewhere in the hospital he could be seen. 9/18 I was contacted that no appts were open and for pt to keep the 10/14 as scheduled and per the provider's note on 9/16 he should see Dr Harsha for an implant evaluation. 9/17 Dr. Esquibel agreed to discuss with his staff customer service and coordination of care when seeing patients of the other assigned dentists. He regretted any missed opportunity to resolve it on the same day until he had an opportunity to discuss with the provider and review the patient's dental history. At his next appt if other that our dental service needs to be involved that will be Dr Harsha's recommendation on next step of care.
Closing Date:	09/19/2014

So to sum this up with Flake's office, I have no use for him or anybody in his office. *Politics?*

37

Over and Out

My book is called *Honorably Dishonored*. I will note the honorable part, and that is my discharge, number one. It also pertains to people and how they treated me. But the dishonorable part, low-class poor excuses for human beings can lie, obtain extra money from the VA because they agree not to perform operations, appointments, procedures, and so on.

This is called the creeping cutback. A good example for this is a movie called *Article 99* starring Ray Liotta, Kiefer Sutherland, Lea Thompson, Forest Whitaker, and Kathy Baker. And finally, at the end of the movie is where the inspector general, starring Noble Willingham, comes to the VA hospital and busts—and I mean busts in half—the director, all of the crooked doctors, and nurses that were abusing the veterans. This is a must-see movie. Even by *you!* All of you non-caring chief of staff, pencil-pushing, money-grubbing low-lives that I'm tired of hearing say, "Thank you for your service" when you don't mean it. Straighten up! Listen to President Donald Trump. *Make America Great Again. Treat a vet good and treat a vet right.*

Great again, do you understand? President Trump says make America great again! Listen to the leader of your country.

Oh yeah, one honorable thing I would like to mention. Dr. Bergen in Neurology at the Tucson VA Hospital, I would like to thank you for supporting our great, great president, Donald J. Trump. I know that when we had our talk, I felt that you stood behind him 110 percent. So again, thank you, Dr. Bergen. See, there are some honorable people in this world. In my book, there will be a list of who I feel have treated me in an honorable way with this hospital.

I can only think of Job in the Bible, Old Testament, New International Version, Job 1:6–22: Job's first test:

> One day the angels came to present themselves before the Lord, and Satan also came with them. The Lord said to Satan, "Where have you come from?" Satan answered the Lord, "From roaming through the earth and going back and forth in it." Then the Lord said to Satan, "Have you considered my servant Job? There is no one on earth like him; he is blameless and upright, a man who fears God and shuns evil." "Does Job fear God for nothing?" Satan replied. "Have you not put a hedge around him and his household and everything he has? You have blessed the work of his hands, so that his flocks and herds are spread throughout the land. But stretch out your hand

and strike everything he has, and he will surely curse you to your face." The Lord said to Satan. "Very well, then, everything he has is in your hands, but on the man himself do not lay a finger." Then Satan went out from the presence of the Lord. One day when Job's sons and daughters were feasting and drinking wine at the oldest brother's house, a messenger came to Job and said, "The oxen were plowing and the donkeys were grazing nearby, and the Sabeans attacked and carried them off. They put the servants to the sword, and I am the only one who has escaped to tell you!" While he was still speaking, another messenger came and said, "The fire of God fell from the sky and burned up the sheep and the servants, and I am the only one who has escaped to tell you!" While he was still speaking, another messenger came and said, "The Chaldeans formed three raiding parties and swept down on your camels and carried them off. They put the servants to the sword, and I am the only one who has escaped to tell you!" While he was still speaking, yet another messenger came and said, "Your sons and daughters were feasting and drinking wine at the oldest brother's house, when suddenly a mighty wind swept in from the desert and struck the four comers of the house. It collapsed on them and they are dead, and I am the only one who has escaped to tell you!" At this, Job got up and tore his robe and shaved his head. Then he fell to the ground in worship and said: "Naked I came from my mother's womb, and naked I will depart. The Lord gave and the Lord has taken away; may the name of the Lord be praised." In all this, Job did not sin by charging God with wrongdoing.

That is the way I, Michael French, feel, and that is the way I feel forever and so on with my great president, Donald J. Trump. For I know he is from God. And you people cannot keep going on this way. If you have not had circumcision in your heart, you need to have it. All of us veterans have fought for you and your families and our country. Why in the world would you continue to treat us this way.

How many demons are there? I have another war to fight with those demons and under God's hand. I will. You will see, and you will feel even more devastation of what can happen to you if you are not always on top of situations in your life. In Volume 2 of *Honorably Dishonored*, which will be coming out soon, the first one hundred people who contacts my publishing company about it will be presented a copy at no cost. I will meet them in person and sign the book for them. Thank you, and God bless you!

Here below is the original and first Hippocratic Oath.

I swear by Apollo Physician and Asclepius and Hygieia and Panaceia and all the gods and goddesses, making them my witnesses, that I will fulfil according to my ability and judgment this oath and this covenant:

To hold him who has taught me this art as equal to my parents and to live my life in partnership with him, and if he is in need of money to give him a share of mine, and to regard his offspring as equal to my brothers in male lineage and to teach them this art—if they desire to learn it—without fee and covenant; to give a share of precepts and oral instruction and all the other learning to my sons and to the sons of him who has instructed me and to pupils who have signed the covenant and have taken an oath according to the medical law, but no one else.

I will apply dietetic measures for the benefit of the sick according to my ability and judgment; I will keep them from harm and injustice.

I will neither give a deadly drug to anybody who asked for it, nor will I make a suggestion to this effect. Similarly I will not give to a woman an abortive remedy.

In purity and holiness I will guard my life and my art.

I will not use the knife, not even on sufferers from stone, but will withdraw in favor of such men as are engaged in this work.

Whatever houses I may visit, I will come for the benefit of the sick, remaining free of all intentional injustice, of all mischief and in particular of sexual relations with both female and male persons, be they free or slaves.

What I may see or hear in the course of the treatment or even outside of the treatment in regard to the life of men, which on no account one must spread abroad, I will keep to myself, holding such things shameful to be spoken about.

If I fulfil this oath and do not violate it, may it be granted to me to enjoy life and art, being honored with fame among all men for all time to come; if I transgress it and swear falsely, may the opposite of all this be my lot.

The classical version of the Hippocratic Oath is from the translation from the Greek by Ludwig Edelstein. From *The Hippocratic Oath: Text, Translation, and Interpretation* by Ludwig Edelstein Baltimore: Johns Hopkins Press, 1943.

ABOUT THE AUTHOR

This book is true and straight from my heart. Ever since I was fourteen years old until when I was sixty two years old. I am writing about the wonderful and precious years when I was a child living in Chicago and working and experiencing a great life. Up until seventeen years of age and still a child entering the Marine Corps, boot camp in Parris Island. After four years in the Marine Corps, from 1973 to 1977, I was home again in Chicago but now so injured from boot camp I couldn't get rid of it. The feelings, the agony, the stress, the dreams. I am going to climb into your mind as you read this book. Feel this book, my experiences will belong to you. Even from 2013 until 2018 my tears will be yours.

Sincerely,

Michael French